Wm. E. Caldwell.

RAMBLES AMONG WORDS:

Their Poetry, History, and Wisdom.

BY

WILLIAM SWINTON, M. A.,

AUTHOR OF "CAMPAIGNS OF THE ARMY OF THE POTOMAC," "DECISIVE BATTLES OF THE WAR," "SCHOOL HISTORY OF THE UNITED STATES," "WORD-ANALYSIS," ETC.

Polonius. What do you read, my lord?
Hamlet. Words, words, words.

SHAKESPEARE.

REVISED EDITION.

NEW YORK AND CHICAGO:
IVISON, BLAKEMAN, TAYLOR, AND COMPANY.
1872.

PREFACE.

THE material of this little book originally appeared in the form of articles contributed to PUTNAM'S MAGAZINE (dear old Maga, with its dress of pea-green and its corn-stalk emblem!) during the years 1853 and 1854. Afterwards the papers were put together in book form, and published in 1858. Since that time the "Rambles" has passed through several editions, and has been reproduced in London with emendations by an English editor. As there is still a certain demand for it, and the book has for some time been out of print, a new edition is now issued by Messrs. Ivison, Blakeman, Taylor, & Co.

It would be strange indeed if, after the score of years that have elapsed since the book was composed, more than half of the score spent in active journalism (than which no schooling is more admirably fitted to take the nonsense out of a man), — it would be strange indeed, if the author had not outgrown his work. When it was written the writer was yet in his teens; and if this be not sufficient excuse for its youthful vices of style, he has none other to offer. Still, it seems that the very enthusiasm and *verve* of the book have had their attractions for students at the age of poetry and faith; and perhaps this may be taken in partial mitigation of its faults.

Such as it is, "with all its imperfections on its head," the RAMBLES is now again given to the public. It is in no wise a book of erudition, but merely a slight contribution to the popular study of our native philology.

W. S.

NEW YORK, 1872.

CONTENTS.

RAMBLE FIRST.

PRELIMINARY.

JOHN STERLING records that when about nine years old he was struck that the word *sincere* was derived from the practice of filling up flaws in furniture with wax, whence *sine cera* came to mean pure, not vamped up. This explanation he says gave him great pleasure and abode in his memory as having first shown him that there is a reason in Words as well as in things.

I suppose many of us are conscious of having made similar pleasurable discoveries. With what exultation have I many a time welcomed the flashing across my mind of the interior import of a word, revealing some deep analogy or subtle beauty or furnishing a new and pungent pointing to some old moral. Nor can I imagine it possible to awaken without a thrill of delight to the first consciousness of such meanings as are wrapt up in 'WRONG,' which is just something *wrung* or distorted from the right—'HEAVEN,' the firmament heaved or *heaven* up over us—'SUBTLE,' whose primary meaning is fine spun—'MISER,' which is just miserable; or learn without a glow of lively satisfaction that 'ABSURD' implies a malappropriate reply such as might come from a *surdus* or deaf man, who, knowing nothing of the antecedents of the conversation, would of course be apt to answer *absurdly;* that a 'CLOWN' is simply a *colonus* or tiller of the ground; that 'SCOUNDREL' conceals in its composition a soldier who ab*sconds* at muster-*roll;* that 'RIVALS' are, etymologically, dwellers on the banks of the same *rivulet* or stream—a circumstance so apt to give rise to quarrels and bickerings; or that 'SYCOPHANT' shuts up a curious piece of Greek history and alludes to persons informing on individuals exporting figs—*syca*—from Attica.

The copiousness of meaning which Words enwrap is indeed more than all that was said or thought. Children of the mind, they reflect the manifold richness of man's faculties and affections. In language is incarnated man's unconscious passionate creative energy. There is an endless, indefinable, tantalizing charm in Words. They bring the eternal provocations of personality. They come back to us with that alienated majesty which a great writer ascribes to our own thoughts.

They are the sanctuary of the intuitions. They paint humanity, its thoughts, longings, aspirations, struggles, failures—paint them on a canvas of breath, in the colors of life.

To the illustration of the opulences of Words I design these pages: with Runic spells to evoke the pagan wanderers from their homes in the visionary eld—to read some of the strange lessons they teach, to catch of the wit and the wisdom, the puns and the poetries, the philosophies, the fancies and the follies that lurk in and flash out from them, and to seize, flaming down, as it were, from the "firmament of bards and sages," some of the deep analogies, the spiritual significance, the poetic beauty and the rich humor that sport and dwell in even our common, every-day words and phrases.

Of course we shall ramble, now chasing some gay etymologic butterfly, anon lingering 'neath the palm and plantain of genius or lonely wandering 'mid

> The intelligible forms of ancient poets,
> The fair humanities of old religion,
> The power, the beauty and the majesty
> That have their haunts in dale or piny mountains,
> Or forest, by slow stream or pebbly spring,
> Or chasms and watery depths.

Medals of the mind we may call words. And as the medals of creation from the Geologic world reveal the workings of creative energy and the successive developments of the divine idea, so Words present a humanitary Geology where histories, philosophies and ethics lie embodied and embalmed. But this is a spiritual Geology, its strata built up of the rich deposits of mind. With passionate fervor man pours himself on nature. An irrepressible longing to express his secret sense of his unity with nature possesses him: and from the consciousness, all plastic and aglow, rush Words, infinitely free, rich and varied, laden with pathos and power, with passion, poetry, humor, thought.

Of course Language is a living Original. It is not made but grows. The growth of language repeats the growth of the plant. At first it is only root: next it puts forth a stem, then leaves, and finally blossoms. "One must not," writes William Von Humboldt, "consider a language as a product dead and formed but once: it is an animate being and ever creative. Human thought elaborates itself with the progress of intelligence; and of this thought language is a manifestation. An idiom cannot therefore remain stationary: it walks, it develops, it grows up, it fortifies itself, it becomes old and it reaches decrepitude."

Language must move with the movements of mind, as the ocean obeys siderial influences. A petrified and mechanical national mind will certainly appear in a petrified and mechanical language. But the provisions are perfect. The renovation of language is provided for, as the renovation of the races is provided for, by a subtle chemistry. The sublime democracy of speech! When a tongue has become dead and effete, the mind walks out of it. With an advance in the national mind—with the influx of a nobler spirit, comes a renovation of its language: by a passionate propulsive movement it ejects its old dead speech, and rises to larger and freer expression. Like the waters in spring, the rising spirit sweeps away the frozen surface of an effete society, literature, language and thought.

The great tidal movements in a nation's life are repeated in great tidal movements in its language. With new creations, thoughts and hopes emerge new demands on the horizon of its speech. The English language shows in its growth crises that mark real upsurgings from the spontaneous depths of human nature. In Chaucer is embalmed that rich primitive sensuous perception of English life, when the language became so opulent in expressions of sensible objects and simple feelings. The flood-tide in the national mind that came with the Sixteenth Century finds expression in the Elizabethan literature, especially in Shakespeare in whom English reached its truly modern mould. And the vast billowy tendencies of modern life, too—the new political, social, scientific births—are making new demands on the English idiom. It is for America especially to evoke new realizations from the English speech. Always waiting in a language are untold possibilities. On the lips of the people, in the free rich unconscious utterance of the popular heart are the grand eternal leadings and suggestions.

Of all the heritages which America receives the English language is beyond all comparison the mightiest. Language of the grand stocks, language of reception, of hospitality, it is above all fitted to be the speech for America. There is nothing fortuitous in language. It is for reasons the English idiom is here. In the English, more than all others, was concentrated the spirit of the modern, breaking up the old crystalline classic mould. It is for America grandly to use this grand inheritance. No language has, no language ever had, such immense assimilation as the English. Freely it absorbs whatever is of use to it, absorbs and assimilates it to its own fluid and flexible substance. This rich copious hospitable flow is to be encouraged.

In the growth of Words all the activities of the

mind conspire. Language is the mirror of the living inward consciousness. Language is concrete metaphysics. What rays does it let in on the mind's subtle workings! There is more of what there is of essential in metaphysics—more of the structural action of the human mind, in Words, than in the concerted introspection of all the psychologists. "In language," observes Frederick Schlegel in a profoundly suggestive passage, "all the principal powers have a nearly equal part and share. The grammatical structure is furnished by the reason. From the fancy, on the other hand, is derived whatever is figurative; and how far does not this reach, extending into the primary and natural signification of words, which often no longer exists, or at least is rarely traceable? And so also that deep spiritual significance, that characteristic meaning, which in the original stem-syllable and radical words of some rich old language, invariably is regarded as a beauty, must be ascribed to the understanding, which so profoundly seizes and precisely designates whatever is peculiar, unless perhaps it is preferred to assign it to an immediate feeling which wonderfully harmonizes with or responds to it."

In our studies on Words, then, a simple logic is indicated for us in the several mental activities that work in the mechanism of speech. Through the portals of the Senses enter the vivid presentings of nature. On these the constructive Reason, the idealizing Imagination, the ethical Conscience work. Of this working words are the records. Hence their warranty. This it is that gives them their authority as profound moral teachers, and amber-like, embalms within them great and noble poetries, histories and philosophies.

It may not be amiss to throw out a few illustrations of the treasures hoarded in Words. Such intimations may serve the office of the overture—that is, may strike fundamental chords.

A law that runs through the warp and woof of language is the familiar principle of a translation of sensible perceptions into the realm of ideas, into metaphysics and morals.

We are all conscious of a psychologic state when the mind is balancing between conflicting possibilities, when, as Dante has it,

Il si e il no nel capo mi tenzoni,

when "Yes and No contend within the head." Now how faithfully has the common intuition embodied this condition in our 'SUSPENSE,' which is indeed the being—suspensus—*hung up*, balancing in deliberation. And its analogue 'DELIBERATION,' which I have just used, follows a like figure—it being just the action of that mental *balance*—libra—into which possibilities and probabilities are thrown. Our word 'AUSPICIOUS' embalms a curious reminiscence of the good omens of the *auspex*, or bird-inspector, whom the old-world nations were wont to consult as oracles; while 'FISCAL' carries a reminder of the *fiscus* or wicker basket which in primitive times contained the revenue of the state. So 'FRUGAL' is strictly fruit-bearing, 'CANDOR' is just whiteness, and 'SERIOUS' (*sine risus*) is the being unable to raise a laugh.

History, too, and vivid and vital history records itself in Words. The coal in my grate is pictured with ferns that flourished untold millennia ago. With equal fidelity national customs, historic events and mighty social revolutions are indelibly stamped on word-medals.

What a curious piece of history does 'PECUNIARY' record! The Latin *pecunia*, wealth, property, gives it to us. Unwrapping it still farther we come to *pecus*, cattle, herds: so that, flocks and herds being in primitive and pastoral times the chief wealth, *pecunia* became afterwards the expression for all the representatives of property. What a strange tale, too, does 'SAUNTER' tell! The Crusades rise at the spell. *Saunt* and *Terre*—the *holy land*—is the composition of the term: and so, literally, a going to the Holy Land.

But as this originally meritorious performance soon degenerated in many cases into the mere pretence for idling and mendicity, the claim of going to the *Saunt terre* came to be regarded as a mere ruse, and 'SAUNTER' took the opprobrious burden it now bears with it. I have here but space to mention the word 'WIFE,' whose etymologic connection with *weave*, *web*, etc., records an interesting piece of primitive socialism.

Nor less has the informing fancy interwoven its fairy imaginings in Words. The Grotesque and Arabesque are here, too. 'HOCUS-POCUS' for instance, is said to be a monkish muddle for *Hoc est corpus Christi* (the formula, *This is the body*, etc.). A 'NOSTRUM' preserves the claim of the Mediæval quacks to their specifics as being—nostrum—*ours*, that is remedies unknown to all the rest of the world: and to be in a 'QUANDARY' is just to be in a pickle where you may well ask, qu'en dira-t-on—*what will they say to it?*

Marvelous are the modes in which the word-forming faculties have labored to give to terms burdens of abuse. The very anatomy of the human passions is to be found here. I may instance 'RASCAL' whose primary signification is, in the words of Verstegan, * an "il favoured leane and woorthelesse deer," and

* Restitution of Decayed Intelligence.

then, by a "strayned sence" applied to a mean vile fellow—the worst of the herd. Genial old Roger Ascham has a pungent illustration of the primary meaning of rascal:

> "A father that doth let loose his son to all experiences is most like a fond hunter [that is, a *foolish* hunter] that letteth slip a whelp to the whole herd; twenty to one he shall fall upon a *rascall* [that is, 'a leane woorthlesse deer'] and let go the fair game."
>
> *The Scholemaster.*

'FANATIC,' too, is well worth exploring. The Roman *fanaticus* was simply one ardently attached to the *fana* or temples. But as these devotees carried their superstitious observances to outrageous lengths, as lacerating themselves with knives, and so forth, the term naturally came to assume the opprobrious meaning it bears with us. As to 'VIXEN' that is just a *fox*-en—she fox, and 'BLACKGUARD' shuts up a curious piece of English history, of which more anon.

The Morals in Words! Language is man's own judge. Minos and Rhadamanthus are here. Terrible the tales they often tell of human frailty and depravity; grand often are they in their beautiful scorn of the mean and ignoble. How fine the allusion conveyed in 'WORSHIP,' which is indeed just one's *worth-ship!* 'DECENT,' too, tells us how *becoming*—decens—is the quality. And what a terrible sentence is heaped on all pride, on

> The boast of heraldry, the pomp of power,
> And all that beauty, all that wealth e'er gave,

in the fact that 'VANITY' (*vanitas*, *vanus*, empty) is but *emptiness!*

I find, however, I am running these premonitory thoughts into the very pith of the book, so here I shall abruptly close. But I read the other day in the Cratylus of Plato an utterance of that old Socratic brain, so subtle, so genial; and which I find after the lapse of these twenty-odd centuries still so authentic and intelligible that I cannot resist transferring it to my page.

"O Hermogenes, son of Hipponicus, there is an old proverb, that beautiful things are somehow difficult to learn. Now the learning relating to *names* happens to be no small affair. I would not myself, Cratylus, confidently assert a single point of what I have said above. But I have considered with Hermogenes in the way it seemed good to me, so that on this account, at least, speak boldly, as I am ready to receive it, if you have anything better to say than this. Nor shall I wonder if you have something to say better; for you seem to me to have considered things of this kind yourself, and to have learned them from others. Should you, then, say anything better, write me down as one of your disciples respecting the meaning of *Words.*"

RAMBLE SECOND.

THE WORK OF THE SENSES.

"Speech is the perfect expression of the Senses. Words are but the representations of the disintegrated body of Man."

OKEN.

SYDNEY SMITH has somewhere an amusing passage illustrative of the radical sensualism that underlies our most supersensual terms, wherein alluding to our æsthetic application of such expressions as 'taste,' 'tact' (from the Latin verb to *touch*), 'eye,' etc., he observes that we will doubtless soon come to speak of a man with a fine 'nose' for this or that province of physics or philosophy.

Extravagance aside, the Senses have certainly left their seal and superscription, sharp, unmistakable, on the words of our language. The rôle they fill in the body forthshadows their part and play in speech. Roots of man's nature—outlets and inlets of the world

—their vivid, strong-flavored presentings run spine-like through language. 'SENSIBLE' is but a lively condition of the *senses* or feelings, 'APATHY' is want of *feeling*—'GUSTO' is an idealization of rich juicy *taste*—'TACT' is delicacy of *touch*, the 'TANGIBLE' is what can be *touched*—'RANK' and 'NASTY' have both a far-off genesis in terms implying the *nose*—and 'ACUTENESS' is properly just sharpness of hearing. How copiously, too, has the Eye contributed! 'CIRCUMSPECTION,' for instance, is a careful *looking* (specio) *around on all sides* (circum), hence mental wariness—'PERSPICUOUS' is what is readily to be *seen through*—and 'ENVY' finely seizes that *askance look* which is the natural manifestation of this passion.

Everywhere man finds *himself*, and builds on the ideals of his own mental structure. Civilization is but the crystallization into fact of the human faculties and functions. The practical arts are but an expanded Hand: telescope and microscope are realizations of the structure of the Eye: he adds boots of swiftness to his feet in railroads and steam navigation: and his nervous system is repeated, after sublime proportions, in the electric threads with which he is now reticulating the planet.

All words are primarily sympathetic. Words are born of a passionate yearning. And it is through the Senses that the mind goes out to nature: these the filaments and outreachings—these the subtle threads that link phenomena and the mind. I find an impressive testimony to this primary law of language in the word 'THOUGHT.' Evidently enough it is an abstraction from the verb to think (Saxon, thencan, past part. thoht), which Horne Tooke* derives from *thing*—I am *thing*-ed, Me thinketh, that is Me *thingeth*—precisely analogous to the Latin 'REOR' from *res*—derivations that may intimate the extent to which *things* color *thoughts.*

It is an interesting illustration of how intellectual conceptions are but a translation of sensible perceptions that the word 'WITS' was formerly used as synonymous with 'SENSES,' a meaning which we can appreciate from the phrase, to be 'OUT OF ONE'S WITS,' that is, to be out of one's senses. It also intimates a curious piece of metaphysics: as though the sole 'source' of wit and wisdom were through the avenues of the senses. In Chaucer I find the following instance of its employment:

"Thou hast don sinne again oure Lord Crist, for certes the three enemies of mankind, that is to sayn, the flesh, the fend, and the world, thou hast suffred hem entre into thin herte wil-

*Diversions of Purley, p. 608.

fully by the windowes of thy body, and hast not defended thyself suffisantly agein hir assautes and hir temptations, so that they han wounded thy soule in five places, this is to sayn, the dedly sinnes that ben entred into thyn herte by thy five *wittes*," etc.

*Tale of Melibeus.**

And how terribly does this passage find realization in our 'SENSUAL,' that is, a devotion of all the powers to the service of the senses—a devotion, which Goethe has embodied with such terrific power in the creation of Mephistophiles.

On the other hand, what a noble compensation is found in the word 'SENSE,' which simply means *feeling*, as though only a man of *feeling* were a man of 'sense.' And certes between the man of noble heart and he of great good sense, there is a close enough connection. To what lofty statement of this thought did Swedenborg rise in his august and oracular utterance that "the quality of one's life is the quality of his love!" And perhaps there is a profounder veracity than we might be apt to suppose in the old maxim: *Quantum sumus scimus*. At least it might do us no harm to have a little more faith in heart-tellings and a little less in the mere dictates of mortality.

* Tyrwhitt's Chaucer, vol. ii. p. 284.

"We live in deeds, not years; in thoughts, not breaths;
In feelings, not in figures on a dial.
We should count time by heart-throbs."

So saith Festus. And so, perhaps, did some of us in the early, purer days when "Heaven lay about us in our infancy," as Wordsworth has it, and before the shades of the prison-house had begun to close upon the growing boy. Then we measured time, not by the rigid exactitude of days and weeks and months and years; but years by the springing of the primrose on the sun-kissed braes; and months and weeks and days, by the exuberance of our emotions,—and that was boundless.

The gustatory propensities of mankind have left significant seals on Words. Thus, we express one of our strongest mental repugnances by 'DISGUST,' that is just 'DISTASTE'; while everything that is unsystematic and chaotic in intellect finds expression in 'CRUDITY' which is simply the being—crudus—*uncooked.* 'PALATE,' also, we employ in the same sense as taste: thus, "men of nice *palates* could not *relish* Aristotle as *dressed up* by the schoolmen." How utterly sensuous! Shakespeare, however, follows in the same direction:

"Devotion, patience, courage, fortitude,
I have no *relish* of them."

Now, of the force of 'RELISH,' we all have a keen enough appreciation; but our unexpressed, passive understanding of it is brought out in finer edge by Minsheu's etymology thereof, from *relecher*—that which is so pleasing to the palate as to tempt one to *lick his lips!*

'CAUSTIC,' 'MORDANT' and 'PIQUANT' have also a like reference to the sense of taste, and sufficiently explain themselves, in their *burning*, *biting* and *stinging* allusions. 'SAUCY' is just *salsus*, salted: 'saucy' talk is therefore talk too highly *peppered* with *salt*—in general, *too* 'spicy.' And 'RACY' always reminds us of the *root* whence it springs. Thus Cowley's

"Rich, *racy* verses in which we
The soil from which they come, taste, smell and see."

'SAVORY' and 'INSIPID' are both from one root—*sapio*, to taste: the one signifying 'tasty' and the other 'tasteless;' while the highest intellectual endowments can result in nothing more exalted than a man of 'SAPIENCE,' which is also just a man of taste. So, too, our Parisians have sublimated their conceptions of all that is highest in modes or morals into their 'BON GOÛT.' But this is not much to be wondered at, since they are constitutionally rather Epicurean in their philosophy; and it is so natural, with the smack of Clos-Vougeot or Chateau-Lafitte on the lips, to transfer the figure, not without *gusto*, to one's æsthetic judgments. However, so be it: since *De gustibus non est disputandum.*

Now besides all this, we are acquainted with at least one northern European nation (not to mention the Chinese), who hold that the soul lies in the *abdomen*, and in whose language those two distinctly divergent facts—soul and stomach, find expression in one and the same term. Moreover the Greek for mind—PHREN—is (what is remarkable for so introspective a race) that which also expresses *midriff* or *diaphragm!*

What a lesson do these words read us on the gastronomic proclivities of our race! Should we not join in the pious ejaculation of Dan Chaucer?

> "Adam, our father, and his wif also,
> Fro Paradis to labour and to wo,
> Were driven for that vice, it is no drede.
> For while that Adam fasted, as I rede,
> He was in Paradis, and whan that he
> Ete of the fruit defended on a tree,
> Anon he was outcast to wo and peine.
> *O glotonie, on thee wel ought us plaine!*"
>
> *The Pardoneres Tale.**

* Tyrwhitt's Chaucer, vol. ii. p. 182.

The contributions from the sense of Sight are numerous and interesting. Nor will they, if questioned, yield less significant replies than such as have just engaged our attention. 'FANCY,' 'PHANTASY' (fantasy), 'FANTASTICAL,' 'PHANTOM,' 'PHANTASM,' 'PHASE' and 'PHENOMENA' are all drawn from the Greek verb to *see* to *seem*, to appear—*phaino:* 'FANCY' and 'PHANTASY' being the image-forming faculty; 'PHANTOM' and 'PHANTASM' mere images, *spectres* (specio, to see); 'PHASE' an aspect, and 'PHENOMENA' being but the apparent, the seeming, in opposition to the absolute, the *real* (*realis*, having relation to *things*—res). 'THEORY' and 'SPECULATION' have an analogous origin, both of them implying a contemplating abstractly, without reference to the practical. Shakespeare furnishes an instance of the use of 'SPECULATION' in its primary sense of sight:

> "Thou hast no *speculation* in those eyes;"

and 'SPECULATION' in its commercial application has reference to the keen *look-out* that is required to take advantage of ups and downs of the market. 'VISIONARY' should be mentioned in the same connection, implying as it does the being given to indulging in mere vague visions. And 'PROVIDENCE' is precisely *fore-sight:* while, applied to deity, it is indicative of

Him whose luminous glance penetrates the farthest abysses of the coming time, and in whose divine scheme all is provided for.

'INTUITION' finely expresses that mental *insight*, that 'MIND'S EYE' that reads omens where it goes and lights up nature with luminous provocations. 'IDEA,' too, is just an *image* or picture formed in the mind through perceptions of sight. But that was a splendid translation which the term received in the hands of Plato when he raised IDEAI to mean the archetypes or patterns existing in the Divine mind, and of which all material forms and embodiments are but projections.

I have already referred to the word 'ENVY' as finely picturing that side-long covetous glance that this passion inspires. 'INVIDIOUS' is precisely the same, with a Latin origin. Nor less pictorial is 'RESPECT,' which its analogue 'REGARD' will well interpret for us. For our 'REGARD' primarily implies a looking at, an observing: so, 'RESPECT' is properly just—respectus—*a looking back.* The metamorphosis they undergo is curious. For a 'respectable' person is just one so worthy of 'regard' as to cause us to *look back again at him!* 'RESPECTABLE' has, however, been sadly degenerating these late years, being now chiefly employed to designate decayed gentility or mental mediocrity.

'SEER,' again, is simply one who *sees*—a *see*-er—whose Eye has been unsealed to the "open secret" of the universe, in Fichte's grand thought—a secret hidden from the wise and prudent (in their own imaginings), and yet 'revealed'—revelo—*unveiled* to those exercising the faith and the humility of babes. Nor does there exist the problem for which benign Nature will not give the response, will we but wisely and trustingly interrogate her. For we know that she

"Never did betray
The heart that loved her."

"The answer lies around, written in all colors and motions, uttered in all tones of jubilee and wail, in thousand-figured, thousand-voiced, harmonious nature; but where is the cunning eye to whom that God-written apocalypse will yield articulate meaning? We sit as in a boundless phantasmagoria and dream-grotto; boundless, for the faintest star, the remotest century, lies not even nearer the verge thereof; sounds and varied-colored visions flit around our sense; but Him, the unslumbering, whose work both dream and dreamer are, we see not—except in rare, half-waking moments, suspect not."

Sartor Resartus.

Sight is the most spiritual of the senses. Through Sight the structure of the world is revealed. Through it the perception of identity, growths, processes, vistas. Hence the breadth of the significance of this sense in the nomenclature of Science. If Sight carries with it the architecture of the world, Sound brings the universal solvent which whirls matter back to primal æther. In melody Nature whispers to man the secret confessions of her plan. Oken asserts that melody is the voice of the universe whereby it proclaims its scheme or its innermost essence. They at least know this who have felt the mystical o'ermastering of Music. Music is a passionate yearning after more primeval natures.

The contributions of the Senses to Words are by no means exhausted. But the principle does not lead far. It is when the creative Reason, the idealizing Imagination begin their work, loading words with new burdens of meaning, that the master-workings of the mind in speech appear. And for a theory of speech somewhat progressive is required.

RAMBLE THIRD.

THE IDEALISM OF WORDS.

"Rendering apparent the images of unapparent natures
And inscribing the unapparent in the apparent frame of the world."
ZOROASTER.

MAN is an idealist. Of this idealism Language is a primitive expression. For Nature, too, is emblematic. There is that subtle consanguinity between Nature and the Soul that the laws of man's mentality have the power to unlock the phenomena of the world. There is a saying reported of Zoroaster, and coming from the deeps of forty centuries, that "the congruities of material forms to the laws of the soul are divine allurements," and that was a sublime audacity of Paracelsus that "those who would understand the course of the heavens above must first of all recognize the heaven in man."

With passionate profusion Nature pours her

splendid solicitations on man. Flood and firmament, light and night, bird and flower, woo him with their sweet eternal persuasions:

> "A rainbow, a sunbeam,
> A subtle smell that spring unbinds,
> Dead pause abrupt of midnight winds,
> An echo or a dream,"—

all speak to the listening soul a strange yet unmistakable language; and to me, even

> "The meanest flower that blows can give
> Thoughts that do often lie too deep for tears."

This idealism of language rests on no whim, but is a primary and necessary fact. Up from the core of nature comes this wondrous symbolism. Words are emblematic because things are emblematic. And as Nature stands the splendid fable of spirit, so the informing Imagination converts the language of outward phenomena into types of the mind. There is no term applied to a metaphysical or moral fact but which, when opened up, is found to be the translation of some fact in nature. 'FERVOR' simply means heat; 'TRACTABLE,' that may be drawn along; 'ABUNDANCE' images an overflowing cup and 'TRANSGRESSION' is the crossing of the line that divides right from wrong. In like manner, when we speak of one's taking 'UMBRAGE' we simply idealize a *shadow*, umbra—the dark *shade* that passes over one's mind. 'SUPERCILIOUS' is a picturesque translation of the act of raising the eyebrows or *supercilium*—the natural expression of hauteur. And a 'SCRUPLE' (of conscience) is a vivid rendering of the *scrupulus* or little bits of gravel that used to get into the very open shoes of the Romans, and produce trouble and hesitancy.

This allegory runs through the warp and woof of language. It is a primary act of the word-forming faculties, which take up a natural symbol and enshrine for ever within it a thought. Let us trace some of the workings of this wondrous law.

What an image of fractious human passions must have filled the mind of that poet who first spoke about 'REFRAINING' therefrom—that is *reining* (frœnum) *them in*, curbing them with bit and bridle! How faithfully, too, is the subtracting one part from a fault and subduing another, thus as it were *thinning it out*, expressed in our 'EXTENUATE' (*tenuis*, thin): and how deep was his knowledge of human nature who first characterized that peering into another's faults and failings as 'SUSPICION.' Could aught be more descriptive, and at the same time convey a better moral, than does 'SCANDAL,' especially when viewed in connection with the Greek *scandalon*, a stumbling-block, or indeed, primarily, a *trap-spring*, a snare? or 'PRECOCIOUS' whose composition implies cooked before the time, as 'PREMATURE' means ripe before the time? or 'OBVIOUS' which is simply so apparent as to meet us—ob vias—in our very way, or 'INSINUATE,' which is just to steal—in sinus—into the breast? We all know the value of 'CANDOR,' but may it not heighten our admiration of the quality when we reflect that a 'candid' man is one whose walk and conversation are—candidus—of *a shining white:* in whose communication is none of the darkness of deceit, but all is fair and lucid? 'DEXTERITY,' again, is sufficiently palpable in all its significations, and yet do we always catch the allusion which plays in the word to the *dextra manus*—the right hand: that is to say, a 'dextrous' person is one whose 'faculties' (that is, *facilities*—the *doing*, the executive part of him) are as perfectly apt and under control as is the right hand of the crafty workman. 'SINISTER,' on the other hand, has relation not to the right or good-omened side, but to the *left* (sinistra) side of the auspex, where ill-omened birds appeared; and so, inauspicious, baleful, adverse. Again, how faithfully is 'PRECIPITANCY' symbolized by that heady haste, which so often causes both persons and projects to *tumble head foremost*—precipitatus! Just as vivid, however, is 'SEDATE' which implies no more of internal repose than can be expressed by a *set* or *set*-tled demeanor—quite closely allied, indeed, to 'DEMURE' which, by the way, is a French quality, claiming descent from *demeurer* to stay, and so some peculiar 'STAIDNESS' (that is, *stay-ed-ness*) of disposition: although it is by no means as cynical as 'MOROSE' for the root of which we need perchance go no deeper than the Latin *moror*, to stay, to loiter.

What chambers of imagery do Words present! Could aught more picturesquely portray that utter indolence and abandon we express in 'SUPINE' than the *lying on the back, with the face upwards*—supinus? or, what could more pungently picture all the burden of significance that dwells in 'SUPPLIANCE' than a bending of the knee (supplex: and so literally a *knee-ling*). 'TRACTABLE' is that may be led along. A 'FRACTIOUS' man is most evidently one who *breaks* loose from all restraint, who *breaks* into fits of passion, etc. An instance of an exceedingly appropriate employment of this word occurs in Struan Robertson's translation of Horace's famous description of Achilles—

"Impiger, iracundus, inexorabilis, acer"—

which he renders into this very pithy and pungent vernacular:

"A fiery Etter-cap, a *fractious* chiel,
As het as ginger, and as stieve as steel!"

Words, too, often make their users instinctive physiognomists. We have seen the allusion 'SUPERCILIOUS' carries with it to the raising of the eyebrows. To the forehead, also, words point as a most expressive feature. Else why do we have such strong terms as 'BROW BEAT,' or 'FROWN' which seems to be contracted from the old French verb frogner—*to knit the brows?* Here the most powerful mental struggles are mirrored, and I recollect Lessing remarks that the reason why the sculptors of the Laocoon did not surround the head with the fillets worn by the priests was to be enabled thus to develop that tremendous expression of agony they have imprinted on the immortal marble.

And more expressive symbols. 'WILD' is *willed, will'd* (or self-willed), in opposition to those, whether men or beasts, who are tamed or subdued, by reason or otherwise to the will of others or of societies*; 'SURD' in Algebra means a quantity *deaf* (surdus) to all attempts at reduction to a rational form; to 'REFLECT' images a *back-casting* of the thoughts; to

* Horne Tooke: Diversions of Purley.

'PONDER' is literally to *weigh*, 'RUIN' finely images mighty *downfall*, 'punctilious' is the observance of every minute *point*—punctillum; and 'IMBECILE' is a forcible metaphor drawn from the old man unable to hobble along without the aid of his *bacillum* or staff!

The law on which this idealism of Words rests has its roots deep in man's mental structure. For as material forms are the revelation of spiritual natures, so the vivid imagination is constantly bringing provocations to ampler translations of our everyday perceptions and experiences. From insight from a large perception of Analogy, from a longing and passionate heart comes the power of thus translating the presentings of nature into the expressive symbols of moral and metaphysical existences. To a sincere and tender nature words lend themselves plastic and willing to the formative laws of the word-forming faculties. Illustrations of the working of these laws run through our and every language. When we speak of a 'cordial' man or manner, is it not plain that we are simply ascribing to the man or manner the quality of being *hearty* (cor, cordis, the *heart*)? 'EGREGIOUS' too is lifted out of its special, definite meaning of the animal chosen—e grege—*out of the flock*, and idealized in a vigorous image to represent any property so remarkable as to remove it from the ordinary rule and mark it as unique and unapproachable. The Latin term *prævaricator*, which originally implied a straddler with distorted legs has given us our verb to 'PREVARICATE,' which we readily perceive has been abstracted to imply a mental or moral *shuffling*. In like manner when Prince Hal addresses Falstaff in the words "How now, my sweet creature of *bombast*," he is using the noun 'BOMBAST' in its literal sense of soft padding used to swell garments: this primary acceptation, however, the word has now entirely lost, and we have transferred it to idealize a swelling, inflated style of talking, fustian—vox et preterea nihil. I see I have used the word 'FUSTIAN' in illustration of 'bombast': it is curious that this term has undergone precisely the same curious metamorphosis.

These changes in the meaning of Words—this ebb and flow of significance—is constantly going on in a live language: and it is no extravagance to say that the moral and mental vitality of a people may be gauged in the quantity and quality of these transformations. For over these transformations the genius of the nation unconsciously presides, and the issues of Words represent issues in the national life and thought. This metaphor and metamorphosis of

Words is exceedingly curious. There is probably nothing in which psychologic laws and the organic workings of the human mind more vividly and vitally reveal themselves than here. For though, to the superficial eye, seemingly lawless and capricious, Words yet bristle with rational thought, while even the most startling metaphor and the wildest poetic image has a law and logic of its own.

Of course in pursuing these Niles and Nigers to their source we find many curious turnings and windings, and many strange regions do they flow through. The cozenage of Words brings out many queer affiliations. 'DEBAUCH' is an instance. It tells us that it was at first merely the attempt to draw a workman de (son) bauche—*from his shop*, and so, to 'debauch' him. 'DELIRIUM' is another. It certainly is so if we derive it from *de lira*, that is, *to make baulks in ploughing*, and so, a mental wandering, or raving. And 'ENTHUSIASM' is enthousiasmos—*possessed by a God*, or the feeling that arises from the idea that one *is* possessed by a God. Spinosa, then, to whom Novalis, on account of his fervency in asserting the divinity of universal Nature (hence our 'PANTHEISM,' that the whole—*pan*—is *God*) gave the appellation of the "God-intoxicated man," perhaps presents us with a striking illustration of the primary meaning of the 'Enthusiast.'

It is interesting, too, to interrogate words with a view to detect those still more marked transformations that frequently take place—how the degrees of praise and blame vary—how they receive burdens of meaning that properly belong not to them—how again they have been shorn of their fair proportions of significance, and often how secondary meanings have overlapped the primary ones.

Nature's works are, we know oft times so overpowering in their effects as to *strike one dumb with amazement*—what we call 'STUPENDOUS,' that is, so impressive as to put one into a stupor with awe. This expression, however, we must consider as even more than metaphorical—our *nil-admirari* philosophy recognizes no such impressions: 'tis an 'Exaggeration' (Exaggero—a *heaping up* of meaning). And yet it is no more *outré* * than a thousand other extravaganzas we are constantly uttering. Thus the slightest possible disturbance we stigmatize as a 'PEST!' or 'PLAGUE!' without any thought of the burden of meaning which the words primarily bear. And yet we hardly 'STIGMATIZE' it either, for that would be *to brand it like a slave*—*stigma* (στίγμα) being originally the mark of Disgrace burned into the brow of a runaway. But indeed,

* French for the Latin 'ULTRA,' beyond.

we are constantly using these heightened metaphors—saying more than we mean. And this Extravagance not only vibrates throughout the general form of phrases and expressions, but discovers itself even in individual words: so that his very language furnishes evidence that man is a creature given to exaggeration. For we cannot even name a 'NUISANCE' (French *nuisance* * from *nuire*, to harm) without averring that it is a positive *injury;* and the slightest 'ANNOYANCE' (also through the Norman *nuire*) we persist in converting into a real *hurt.* Again, what was to the Roman a *fighting against*—repugnantia—has been by us softened down to a mere 'REPUGNANCE;' a *death-struggle*—reluctor—has sunk into the tame 'RELUCTANCE,' and what was once actually *deadly*—perniciosus—has been metamorphosed into the simple 'PERNICIOUS.' Our peaceful 'DEBATE' (de and battre, *to beat down*) was to the Norman—who was more skilful in the use of his sword th an of the weaponsdrawn from the armory of wit—a downright *battle;* while the mild 'LYCEUM' was the Greek's—λύκειον—*wolf's den!* Surely we give

* Happily the letters of this word still continue their allegiance, for which we have *not* to thank Webster—who, following the precedent of Blackstone, recommends that it be spelled *nusance,* though on what principle, except that of "darkening wisdom," it might be difficult enough to determine.

many a command that is not at all deadly either in its nature or consequences, and yet we will call such 'PEREMPTORY.' We may easily be 'astonished,' without being struck with *tonnère*, thunder--or as we say, *thunderstruck*. And it is certainly quite possible for one to be very much 'MORTIFIED' (*mors, mortis*—death) without its proving the *death* of him!

But, while our language furnishes us with instances in which conventional usage has conspired to soften down the too expressive primitive power of words, we on the other hand meet with numerous cases in which terms acquire burdens of significance which primitively and properly belong not to them. The sons become stronger and wiser and wittier than their sires. This we will have occasion to see copiously illustrated hereafter: in the mean time take a few terms wherein we may mark the steps of a progressive civilization. 'TOILET,' for example, cannot, with all its arts, conceal from us the fig-leaved condition that lurks in and peeps out from it; we discern shreds of the *toile*—the mere piece of cloth—which the savage was wont to wrap around his loins to cover him withal and lo! *his* 'toilet' was made! And so the jeweled 'DIADEM' owes its origin to the simple woolen fillet—diadema—which the king, in patriarchal days, bound around his brows; a 'ROBE' is cousin-german to *rob:* the primitive rude, self-helping men *robbed* from the lion or the bear or the wolf his hide—de-*spoiled* him as we say, exultingly cast it about his own shoulders and so the man was the richer by his 'robe' and the beast the poorer by his skin! Nay, 'SCEPTRES' were originally but *willow-wands* and the 'THRONE' itself is but a *chair*;—nay, merely a *stool*, as our humble Saxon progenitors had it. *

'TABERNACLE,' again, is another word with a humble enough origin—being primtively a mere *tabernaculum*, a tent or hut. 'PARADISE' to the oriental was simply a *park* or pleasure-ground. So, too, 'FISCAL' unmistakably points to the fiscus, or wicker basket which, in early times contained the revenue of the State.† A 'FURLONG' was once a *furrow-long*, or length of a furrow; a field of any size was once termed an 'ACRE' (German *acker*); 'DRACHM' in the elder Greek meant a handful, and 'MYRIAD' any great number. And when Homer alludes to a certain Hero

* See King Alfred's Translation of *Boethius de Consolatione Philosophiæ.*

† So to 'CONFISCATE' is evidently to put, forcibly, one's possessions in along with (*con*) what is in the basket (*fiscus*) or hamper of the State—"to adjudge to be forfeited to the public treasury." Webster.

counting his sheep, he employs the expression πεμπεσθαι, etc.,—he *fived* them—showing that their five fingers were originally the limits of their arithmetical notions. And whether or not there be any connection between *deka* (ten) and *duo echo*,* or between *pente* (five) and *panta* (all), our 'DIGIT' (Latin digitus, a *finger*) at least gives a strong confirmation to the supposition; while 'CALCULATE' clearly tells of the *calculi*, or pebbles which the ancients employed to assist them in their arithmetical difficulties.

A ludicrous example of this same attempt to tint things up *couleur de rose* is furnished in the word 'PAMPER,' a term which the Italians have given us—being, I believe, in their language *pambere*, that is, 'pane,' *bread*, and 'bere' *drink*—so that it was originally nothing more luxurious than *bread and drink*, plenty even of that, however, being considered as enough to 'pamper' one. Just as the French *viande*, meat, flesh, becomes our English 'VIANDS' which carries the idea of something more dainty still!

Again that French verb *affronter* which merely implies a meeting face to face—a coming up, *ad frons*, to the forehead, without any necessary hostility—gives

* Just as I have seen it stated that the Gothic *Teiga*, tein, our 'TEN' is just *tai-hun* that is *two hands!* But Tooke is more rational.

us our 'AFFRONT,' with all its causticity of application. We said it did not necessarily imply hostility. Shakespeare suggests numerous examples of its employment in this neutral sense. Thus, in Hamlet, the King says:

> "For we have closely sent for Hamlet hither;
> That he, as 'twere by accident, may here
> *Affront* [that is, simply, may *meet*] Ophelia."
>
> *Hamlet* III. 1.

And indeed it would seem impossible for us irascible Saxons to have even an 'ENCOUNTER' without converting it into a downright battle. A 'MEETING' almost always conveys the idea of something sinister hidden beneath it. And we cannot have even the slightest cause of complaint—*querela*—without picking a 'QUARREL' out of it!

It may be worth noticing in this connection, the feelings, embalmed in language, which have given rise to words expressive of Grandeur and Pettiness—may we not read therein a curious piece of man's mind? There seems to have been all along a very natural, yet rather ludicrous association of grandeur and pettiness with mere physical greatness or littleness. Thus our metaphorical 'GRAND' is simply the French *grand* —implying merely tall, large; while their *petit*, or little, become our 'PETTY' which is less still.* But, indeed, there is something so impressive and imposing about bodily bigness, that we wonder not that those old heroic Normans (or Northmen) *did* appear very '*magni*ficent,' with their great *tallness*—what they called 'HAUTEUR' (haut, *high*), which, alas, all too soon degenerated into mere 'HAUGHTINESS;' or that their 'MAJESTIES,' 'HIGHNESSES,' 'MAGNATES' and 'GRANDEES' should soon have absorbed all nobility and authority.

Often, too, has man tried to gild over his vices with a fine name, calling those 'GALLANTS' who have no claim to the title, giving to persons whose sad life can be gilded with but few rays of genuine joy the appellation of 'FILLES DE JOIE,' covering a blackleg with the mantle of 'CHEVALIER D'INDUSTRIE,' and declaring that a 'PARAMOUR' is one who is loved—par amour—*very affectionately*,† although, by the way, Flute, the bellows-mender, understood the matter better than that:

"*Flute.* He hath simply the best wit of any handicraft man in Athens.

* French *bigness* (gros, grosse), however, degenerates into English 'GROSSNESS,' a fact of curious historic significance.

† And see it used in this good sense throughout the whole of our old English literature.

Quince. Yea, and the best person too: and he is a very *paramour* for a sweet voice.

Flute. You must say, 'PARAGON:' a *paramour* is, God bless us, a thing of naught."

Midsummer Nights' Dream IV. 2.

On the contrary words often do not get their due, and debts which they never contracted are laid to their account. A 'LIBEL,' for instance, is properly just a *libellus*, a little book—what we call a *pamphlet:* as if it would insinuate that the only purpose of such is to defame and malign! So a 'LEGEND' is simply something *to be read*—legendum;* while 'REVEREND' evidently declares that it *ought to be revered*—reverendus; and a 'MAXIM' affirms that it is—maximum —of the greatest importance. So 'CATER,' which is coming with us to acquire a somewhat contemptuous meaning, has no such stain on its birth—it is simply to buy or purchase (*acheter*) for one. So I find in Ben Jonson

"He is my ward-robe man, my *acater*, cook,
Butler and steward."

The Devil an Ass I. 3.†

* For the corruption of this word see Tooke's Diversions of Purley.

† Here the word is *acater*, which is nearly the original form, and yet in Chaucer I find it *achator* (Canterbury Tales 570 et passim) which is nearer still.

'OBSEQUIOUS' is another instance of this same downward tendency in words. For primitively the word has no opprobrious import, signifying simply following after, a meaning which becomes present from our use of 'OBSEQUIES' which is just the *following* the dead to the tomb; and in the elder dramatists we frequently meet with this primary application of 'obsequious.' Thus Shakespeare

> "How many a holy and *obsequious* [that is funereal] tear
> Hath dear religious love stolen from mine eye,
> As interest of the dead."
>
> *Sonnet XXXI.*

Now, however, we employ it but to express that cringing compliance that leads one to *follow* after the favor or fancy of another, or shape one's principles or practice according to his whims. And lastly I may mention the term 'GOSSIP' which tells a strange story: for originally it was just the name applied to sponsors at baptism—literally *God-sibb:* 'sibb,' *related* (to the child, in or through) *God!* Verstegan makes the matter clear:

"Our Christian ancestors understanding a spirituall affinity for to grow betweene the parents, and such as undertooke for the childe at baptisme, called each other by the name of *God-sib*, which is as much as to say as that they were *sib* together, *i.e.* of kin together through God."

Restitution of Decayed Intelligence, C. 7.*

But, while we have, on the one hand, words which have strengthened, and on the other hand, words which have softened and degenerated in signification, we have also words which have completely changed meaning—perfect turn-coats: not mere renegades, as are the others, but downright deserters.

How amazed, for instance, would one of our sturdy old English writers be, were he told, by some modern, tea-imbibing dame that she was very '*nervous*.' Viewing the word from the Latin stand-point—seeing in it merely the classic *nervosus*, *sinewy*, 'muscular'—an epithet only applicable to the stalwart strength of manhood, and which even we can appreciate from the employment of our '*nervous* style,'—we can easily

* Webster bungles over this word. Verstegan would have enlightened him, or Junius either, for that matter. For, as Junius remarks, these *gossips* under cloak of this 'SPIRITUALL AFFINITY' used often to meet to tell stories and . . . . . tipple over them!—a circumstance from which we in English derive our expression 'TO GO A GOSSIPING' etc. And it is a curious coincidence that the French for 'gossip' is *commérage* from commère, a god-mother—a precisely analogous process having taken place in the word.

imagine how the worthy would be either petrified (even though he might *not* be turned into—petra—stone) with amazement; or at least he would regard the good lady as indulging in a joke!* And how much of Carlyle's teaching is but a fiery plaint of the sad seduction so painfully visible in the abysmal gulf that has come to intervene between 'KEN' and 'CAN' —which, we are aware, were once one and the same. But this was before 'CANNING' had become *cunning;* or 'CUNNING' had grown synonymous with *crafty.* So that then the Baconian apothegm, Knowledge is Power was to them a mere truism: since it only asserted that *Ken*-ning is *Can*-ning!

How titanic is the power which many words wield! Indeed, in numerous instances, so terrible is the in-

* In regard to this term Pegge says: "A word which till lately when applied to a man was expressive of Muscular strength, and a Brawny make; and thence metaphorically a strong and forcible style is called *nervous* and energetic: whereas now it is used only, in a contrary sense, to express a man whose nerves are weak, and absolute enervation."

Anecdotes of the Eng. Lang. page 264.

For this corrupt usage, he proposes *nervish!*

Bailey, in his Dictionary gives it in its primitive signification of strength and vigor—and says that when applied to persons of weak nerves it is a "medical cant."

fluence they exercise that mankind has been compelled to break away in affright from their sway into the domain of others less potent. Of this we have a well-known instance in that dangerous African cape, ever so fatal to mariners, and which the wrathful "Spirit of the Cape" lashes into foaming fury. Long was it all too truthfully known by the name of the "Cape of Storms;" but this was to recognize the danger (whereas the feared and the fearful must ever be *nameless*); and so, buoying up their courage, they gave it the more cheerful appellation of the "Cape of Good Hope." Again, how chilling to the ardor of the soldier must be that word 'FORLORN-HOPE'—men sent on a service attended with such peril that hope must be—*forlorn*—relinquished, left behind by them.

But it is in Poetry's mightier idealizations that a far loftier idealism discloses itself—in tones drawn by the Master's hand from the lyre of humanity—in the wild ravings of an old un-Kinged Lear, in an Othello's bursts of wailing sadness or tempestuous madness—

"My wife! my wife! what wife?—*I have no wife!*"

Or, when Cleopatra, refering to the *asp*, says:

"———— Peace, Peace!
Dost thou not see my baby at my breast,
That sucks the nurse asleep?"

Or when with the true prerogative of genius—to marry the phenomena of nature with the moods of man's mind—Shakespeare sees types of insanity in the green scum of the standing-pool—Poor Tom

> "Drinks the green mantle of the standing pool!"

'Tis in the loftier and serener empyrean of Poetry that we catch lineaments—shadowy and far away—of a supernal beauty that haunts and will not leave us and hear tones of more than mortal pathos and power.

> "In the silence of the night
> How we shiver with affright,"

at memories awakened perchance by some one weak word—weak, yet winged: a mere breathing, and yet vitalized by the very spirit of life. And so, under the guidance of Bishop Hutchinson, let us return: "And to make short of this argument, we doubt not but many wise men have too mean an opinion of the power of words and take too little care about them: for though the words of a fool are little, the words of a wise man are wonderful. Words are the judges of our thoughts, the land-marks of all interests; and the wheels of our human world are turned by them. They move interests that are greater than mountains, and many a time have subdued kingdoms. Riches and

Poverty, Love and Hatred, and even Life and Death are in the power of the tongue, and when their effects are least they are still the character of the mind and abilities of him who speaks them; and when they are first and natural, though plain and unaffected they carry charms that are superior to the beauty of the fairest face, while the improper use of them shows ignorance of words that are understood by others, they lessen the man and make the picture as mean as sign-post painting." *

'TRANSIENT' is a suggestive word. It is transiens—*passing away!* With plaintive sadness it sings the requiem of human life. Said Ina's queen, "Are not all things, are not we ourselves like a river hurrying heedless and headlong to the dark ocean of illimitable time?" And I find in the *Romaunt of the Rose* this antique rhyme, through which the same figure runs:

"The time that passith night and daie,
And restilesse travailith aie,
And stelith from us privily,
That to us semith sikirly
That it in one poinct dwellith ever,
And çertes it ne restith never,
But goëth as fast and passeth aie

* From a curious old tract, entitled, "The Many Advantages of a Good Language to any Nation."

That ther n'is man that thinkin maie
What time that now present is,
Askith at these grete clerkis this;
For men thinken redily
Thre timis ben ypassed by
The time that maie not sojourn,
But goth and maie never returne,
As watir that doune runnith aie,
But never droppe returne maie."

How sublime is the allusion in 'NATURE' (*natus*, *natura*, to be born), *the being born*, or indeed the reference in Latin is to the future, as though it would indicate that she is no dead mass, but a living and ever-evolving Whole. And indeed she is our mother, too—nourishing us tenderly on her breast, shedding around us her balmy, balsamic influences, and gently at last rocking us to sleep with sphere-music and old eternal melodies. Shelley, her loveliest and lornest child, shall sing her pæan.

"Mother of this unfathomable world!
Favour my solemn song, for I have loved
Thee ever, and thee only; I have watched
Thy shadow, and the darkness of thy steps,
And my heart ever gazes on the depth
Of thy deep mysteries. I have made my bed
In charnels and on coffins, where black death
Keeps record of the trophies won from thee,

Hoping to still these obstinate questionings
Of thee and thine, by forcing some lone ghost,
Thy messenger, to render up the tale
Of what we are. In lone and silent hours,
When night makes a weird sound of its own stillness,
Like an inspired and desperate alchymist
Staking his very life on some dark hope,
Have I mixed awful talk and asking looks
With my most innocent love, until strange tears,
Uniting with those breathless kisses, made
Such magic as compels the charmed night
To render up thy charge : and though ne'er yet
Thou hast unveiled thy inmost sanctuary;
Enough from incommunicable dream,
And twilight phantasms, and deep noon-day thought,
Has shone within me, that serenely now
And moveless, as a long-forgotten lyre
Suspended in the solitary dome
Of some mysterious and deserted fane
I wait thy breath, Great Parent, that my strain
May modulate with murmurs of the air,
And motions of the forests and the sea,
And voice of living beings, and woven hymns
Of night and day, and the deep heart of man!"

ALASTOR.

RAMBLE FOURTH.

FOSSIL POETRIES.

"Language is fossil poetry. The Etymologist finds the deadest word to have been once a brilliant picture. As the limestone of the continent consists of infinite masses of the shells of animalcules, so language is made up of images or tropes, which now, in their secondary use, have long ceased to remind us of their poetic origin."

EMERSON.

ALL words are, more or less, poetry. For word-making is an organic creation of the mind and runs parallel with the processes of nature and is the crown and consummation of the world. The Hindûs, in their free and fluent mythology, conceived the second act of Brahma to have been the Naming: and it is reported of Pythagoras that he thought that of all wise men he was not only the most rational but also the most ancient who gave the names to things. The poet is by divine right the proper Namer. Through sympathy with the grand substantial Words of the world he imports into human speech the utterance of orphic Nature. Material forms—ocean, air, soil, fire, stars, life, growths—these are sublime primeval Words. These the Expressive passion dissolves into plastic symbols. And the poet gives voice to mankind.

O, shining trails of bards and builders! "Thinkest thou there were no poets till Dan Chaucer?" asks Thomas Carlyle—"No heart burning with a thought which it could not hold, and had no word for, and needed to shape and coin a word for,—what thou callest a metaphor, trope, or the like? For every word we have, there was such a man and poet. The coldest word was once a glowing new metaphor, and bold questionable originality. My very *attention*, does it not mean an *attentio*, a *stretching-to?* Fancy that act of the mind, which all were conscious of, which none had yet named,—when this new poet first felt bound and driven to name it! His questionable originality, and new glowing metaphor, was found adoptable, intelligible, and remains our name for it to this day."

Words are often the expressed essence of poetry—redolent as flowers in spring. 'AURORA' comes to us a snatch of that flowing Grecian Mythus that idealized universal nature; and even to us is she the "rosy-fingered daughter of the morn"

Ηριγένεια ῥοδοδάκτυλος Ἠώς!

And 'MORN,' too, is a sweet poem, coming to us from an old Gothic verb *Mergan*, to dissipate, to disperse: so that the meaning of 'morn' (as also 'morning' and 'morrow') is just the time when darkness is *dissipated, dispersed:*

> "The nyght is passed, lo the *morrowe* graye,
> The fresshe *Aurora* so fayre in apparance
> Her lyght dawith, to voyde all offence
> Of wynter nyghtes."
>
> *Lyfe of our Lady.*

'LETHE' is another classicism: 'tis the river of *forgetfulness*—"the oblivious pool." What a romance in 'Hyperborean'—that is, beyond the region of *Boreas*—where dwelt a pious and happy race: said to be a Homeric creation. 'LEVANT,' 'ORIENT,' and 'OCCIDENT,' are all poems. And so is that noble Saxon 'MAIN,' that is the—*Mægen—strong one:*

> ———"A shepherd in the Hebrid isles
> Placed far amid the melancholy *main.*"

The 'DAISY' has often been cited as fragrant with poesy: 'tis the *day's eye* (Saxon, *daeges ege*). Chaucer has these affectionate lines:

> "Of all the floures in the mede
> Than love I most these floures of which I rede,
> Such that men call *daisies* in our town,
> To them I have so great affectioun ——"

Nor is he alone in his love for the

> "Wee, modest, crimson-tippet flower!"

Quite an odoriferous etymologic bouquet might we cull from the names of Flora's children. What a beauty in 'PRIMROSE' which is just the *prime-rose*, the *first* rose; the 'SWEET WILLIAM;' the 'MORNING GLORY,' except when a pompous classical terminology would convert it into a *convolvulus!* How many sweet associations cluster around the 'FORGET-ME-NOT,' around the 'ANEMONE' (*anemos*, the wind-flower) into which Venus changed her Adonis! Again is there not poetry in calling a certain family of minute crustacea—whose two eyes meet and form a single spot in the centre of the head—'CYCLOPS?' And if any one thinketh there cannot be poetry even in the technicalities of science let him remember

'CORAL' which in the Greek means a *sea damsel*, or the chemical 'COBALT' which is said to be the German Kobold, a *goblin*, the demon of the mines: so called by miners from its being troublesome to work. To be sure Science is a terrible destroyer of these fine phantasies. But,

> "Still the *heart* doth need a language, still
> Doth the old instinct bring back the old names.'

> "There shall be no more *magic* nor *cabala*,
> Nor *Rosicrucian*, nor *Alchemic* lore,
> Nor fairy fantasies; no more *hobgoblins*,
> Nor *ghosts*, nor *imps*, nor *demons*. *Conjurors*,
> *Enchanters*, *witches*, *wizards*, shall all die
> Hopeless and heirless; their divining arts,
> Supernal or infernal—dead with them!"
>
> *Bailey's Festus.*

The 'Student's' prediction is indeed fully verified; and yet must it not have been a terrible reality which could leave so large a precipitate as this, from the alembic?

We are not apt, in this practical age, to be very profoundly devoted to astrolatry, and yet do we ever 'CONSIDER' without holding commerce with the—

*sidera**—stars? The planets, with their heavenly houses, are now to us all mute and motionless—with

"No real voice nor sound;"

and yet is not one man '*mercuri*al;' another '*jovi*al;' a third '*marti*al' and a fourth '*saturn*ine' according as the planet rules his destiny? We are not very much given to erecting figures of the Heavens, and determining 'horoscopes' (*horoskopos*, and so, literally, the observing the hora or *hour* of one's birth—that being necessary in casting a 'nativity):' and yet are not our fortunes sometimes in the 'ascendant;' are there not those who are 'ill-starred,' meet we not with 'dis-*asters*?' And 'INFLUENCE,' too, looks back to a time when the stars shot their sweet impartings to man's heart. So even the nonchalant Frenchman persists in talking about his 'bon-*heur*' and his 'mal-*heur*'—which, of course, we recognise as being naught other than a good or bad *hour*—a good or bad *horoscope*. Perhaps may there be more truth than one might be apt to suppose in this quaint passage from

* The word *may* indeed be from *consido;* as Webster asserts it *is*. But it is characteristic of our worthy lexicographer to lean towards the more unpoetical of disputed derivations—necessary result of his absurd theory of radices.

Chaucer—which sounds forth here like a fragment of some antique ritual:

"Peraventure in thilke lerge book
Which that men clepe the Heven ywritten was
With sterres, when that he his birthe took,
That he for love shuld han his deth, alas!
For in the sterres, clerer than is glas
Is writen, God wot, who so coud it rede,
The deth of every man withouten drede,
In sterres many a winter ther beforn
Was writ the death of Hector, Achilles,
Of Pompey, Julius, or they were born
The strif of Thebes, and of Hercules,
Of Sampson, Turnus, and of Socrates
The deth; *but mennes wittes ben so dull*
That no wight can wel rede it at the full."

The Man of Lawes Tale.

And so Emerson tells us that,

"The old men studied magic in the flowers,
And human fortunes in Astronomy,
And an omnipotence in Chemistry."*

But the age of Faith, like the age of Chivalry, has gone by. We have dissolved partnership with yon

* Emerson's Poems: "Blight."

starry world: the spheral harmonies reach not our dull ears.

So too, have gone trooping back to the land of oblivion the 'GNOMES' and the 'IMPS' (surely nothing very terrible, since the word meant primarily merely a shoot or scion—a *son*); and the 'DEMONS' (who were at first *gods*); and the 'GHOSTS'* and the 'GHOULS' and the 'GENII:'

> "And there were wandering on the highest mountains of Yemen visionary forms—and they described them by the names of *Dogin* or *Genii*, *Ghouls* or *Demons*."†

'CHARM,' 'INCHANT' and 'INCANTATION' all trace their genesis to the time when spells were in vogue. 'CHARM' is just *carmen*, from the fact of a sort of runic rhyme having been used in this sort of diablerie. So 'FASCINATION' recalls the era when the blight of the *evil eye* was an object of terror. By the way

* By the way our quite *un*-ghostly 'GAS' is from the same root—German *geist*, to rush, to blow—*spirit*.

† From a cabalistic enough MS (referred to in the Account of the MSS in the Bibliothèque du Roi), with the following magnificent title: "The Golden Meadows and the Mines of Precious Stones, by Aboul-hassan-Aly, son of A-Khair, son of Aly, son of Abderrahman, son of Abdallah, son of Masoud-el-Hadheli surnamed Masoudi."

'SPELL' means simply *word.* Says Sir Thomas Browne:

> "Some have delivered the polity of spirits, that they stand in awe of charms, *spells*, and conjurations, letters, characters, notes and dashes."

Note, too, that from spell we get our 'GOSPEL,' that is *God's spell*—God's word.

To conclude all of which, take the following exquisite passage from that most etherial "Undine" of De la Motte Fouqué. (By the way is not *Undine* from *unda*, a wave: that is a *water-sprite?*): "You must know, that there are beings in the elements, which bear the strongest resemblance to the human race, and which, at the same time, seldom become visible to you. The wonderful salamanders sparkle and sport among the flames; deep in the earth the meagre and malicious gnomes pursue their revels, the forest-spirits belong to the air and wander in the woods; while in the seas, rivers and streams live the wide-spread race of water-spirits. These last beneath resounding domes of crystal, through which the sky appears with sun and stars, inhabit a region of light and beauty; lofty coral trees glow with blue and crimson fruits in their gardens; they walk over the pure sand of the sea, among infinitely variegated shells, and amid whatever of beauty the old world possessed, such as the present is no more worthy to enjoy; creations which the floods covered with their secret veils of silver; and now those noble monuments glimmer below, stately and solemn and bedewed by the water which loves them and calls forth from their crevices exquisite moss-flowers and enwreathing tufts of sedge."

It is not alone in Oriental tale that speakers drop pearls: we can scarcely open our lips without giving utterance to some rich primitive poetic allusion. On what a grand perception of this wondrous frame, with its boundless unity in variety, is that Greek word 'KOSMOS' formed (the creation is ascribed to Pythagoras), signifying as it does *harmonic order!* So the 'BRUNT' of the battle is just where the battle *burns* hottest; and the 'WELKIN' (Saxon *wealcan*, to roll) is that which rolls over our heads!

The 'halcyon' days! What a balmy serenity in the name! And its fitness becomes the more apparent when we pierce to the secret the word enwraps. The *Alkuon* was the name applied by the Greeks to the Kingfisher. Literally it implies *sea-conceiving*, from the fact of the bird's laying her eggs in rocks near the sea, and the "ἀλκυονιδες ξκδιζμ"—the *halcyon days*—were the fourteen days during the calm weather about the winter solstice during which the bird was said to build her nest and lay her eggs.

The *palm* being to the oriental of such passing price, at once food and shelter, we can easily imagine how he would so enhance its value as to make it the type of every thing prosperous and flourishing. Hence our 'PALMY.' Sir Walter Raleigh has this passage:

"Nothing better proveth the excellency of this soil than the abundant growing of the palm trees without labour of man. This tree alone giveth unto man whatsoever his life beggeth at nature's hand."

'STYLE' and 'STILETTO' might seem radically very different words; and yet they are something more than even cousins-german. 'STYLE' is from the stylus, which the Greeks and Romans employed in writing on their tablets; and as they were both sharp and strong they were capable of being made a very formidable weapon. Cæsar himself, it is supposed, got his quietus by means of a stylus. Many who have felt the bitter, biting tooth of 'SARCASM' will hardly be disposed to consider it a metaphor, even should we trace it to the Greek *sarkazo—to tear the flesh off—literally* to 'flay.' 'SATIRE' again, has an arbitrary enough origin. It is *satira* from satur, mixed: the process of derivation being as follows.

Each species of poetry, among the Romans, had its own special kind of versification; thus, the hexameter was used in epics, the iambic in the drama, etc. Ennius, however, the earliest Roman 'satirist,' first disregarded this conventionality, and produced a *medley* (satur) of all kinds of metre. It afterwards lost this idea of a melange, and acquired the notion of a poem directed against the vices and follies of men.

How few who use that very vague word 'AMBROSIAL' are conscious of the intimation it throws out of the 'ambrosia' (*ambrotos*, immortal)—the food of the gods. It afterwards came to be used in the sense of a perfume, hence fragrant; and that is the primary idea of our 'ambrosial'—instance Milton's 'ambrosial flowers.' The Immortals in the golden halls of 'many-topped Olympus' would seem to have led a merry enough life of it with their nectar and ambrosia:

> "And he kept pouring out for all the other gods, drawing nectar from the goblet. And then inextinguishable laughter arose among the immortal gods, when they saw Vulcan bustling about through the mansion."
>
> *Iliad, Book* I.

But not half as jolly were they as Thor, Odin, and the Northern braves, dead drunk over their mead (*meda*, honey,) and ale, from

"The ale cellars of the Jotun
Which is called Brimir."

Voluspa.

'SERENADE' wafts us away to that bright Italian land, where underneath the *serene* sky

Nox erat, et cœlo fulgebat Luna *serena*
Inter minora sidera,

the lover pours forth his amorous ditties, on the odorous wings of the balmy air, to the ear of his mistress and the Night! A passage from the older editions of Milton will present us with the original orthography of the word:

"———Nor in court amours,
Mixt dance, or wanton mask, or midnight bal,
Or *serenata*, which the starved lover sings
To his proud fair, best quitted with disdain."

Paradise Lost IV. 767.

And Bacon gives the following account of the origin of the word 'CALAMITY:'

"Another ill accident is drouth, at the spindling of the corn; which with us is rare; but in hotter countries common: insomuch as the word *calamitas*, was first derived from *calamus*, *when the corn coulde not get out of the stalke.*"

Natural History.

This Etymology is at best dubious; nay, it is altogether probable that it will have to be quite abandoned. And yet there is a good degree of vraisemblance in the word, for what *could*, in an agricultural community, be a greater 'calamity' than this?

The word 'HEALTH' wraps up within it—for, indeed, it is hardly a metaphor—a whole world of suggestion. It is that which *healeth* or causeth to be whole—what the Scotch call *hale:* that is, perfect 'health' is that state of the man when there is no discord or division in the system, but when all the functions conspire to make a perfect one or *whole.* Carlyle makes a most effective use of this word.

"So long as the several elements of life, all fitly adjusted can pour forth their movement like harmonious tuned strings, it is a melody and unison; Life, from its mysterious fountains, flows out as in celestial music and diapason,—which also like that other music of the spheres, even because it is perennial and complete, without interruption and without imperfection might be fated to escape the ear. Thus, too, in some languages, is the state of health well denoted by a term expressing unity: when we feel ourselves as we wish to be, we say that we are *whole.*"

Characteristics.

O, what a wealth of truth and beauty lies in even our every-day, fire-side words! And what a fragrance have even dry roots!

Every nation has its legend of a Golden Age, when all was young and fresh and fair, "Comme les couleurs primitifs de la nature," ere the shadow of Sorrow—the shadow of ourselves—had stretched itself over life: a morn of Saturnian rule, when gods walked and talked with men. And even now, in spite of our atheism and our apathism, amid the Babel-din of the great Living Present, the solemn voices of the Past return with soft wailings of pity. In the moonlight of memory they revisit us, those visions!

The rainbow comes and goes,
And lovely is the rose;
The moon doth with delight
Look round her when the heavens are bare;
Waters on a starry night
Are beautiful and fair;
The sunshine is a glorious birth;
And yet I know, where'er I go
That there hath passed away a glory from the Earth!

'Tis the mild, Brahminical Wordsworth that sings. Wordsworth, it will be remembered, in that glorious ode—the "Intimations of Immortality from the Recollections of early Childhood"—develops the Platonic idea (shall we call Platonic the thought born of every fine spirit?) of *Anamnesis*—of a shadowy recollection of past and eternal existence in the profundities of the divine heart. "It sounds forth here a mournful reminiscence of a faded world of gods and heroes—as the echoing plaint for the loss of man's original celestial state and paradisiacal innocence." *

And then come those transcendent lines that are borne to us like aromatic breezes blown from the Islands of the Blest.

> "Hence in a season of calm weather
> Though inland far we be,
> Our souls have sight of that immortal sea,
> Which brought us hither—
> Can in a moment travel thither,
> And see the children sport upon the shore
> And hear the mighty waters rolling ever more!'

But,

> "descending
> From those imaginative heights that yield
> Far-stretching views into Eternity"—

what have Golden Ages and Platonisms to do with our word-strolls? A good deal. For language as the mirror of the inmost consciousness may illustrate both.

Why is it that we generally speak of Death as a *return* or a *return home;* and how is it that the same

* Frederick Schlegel: *Philosophy of Life.*

thought has interwoven itself with the very warp and woof of our speech and song? So 'decease' but implies a withdrawal; 'demise' a removal. It is curious to trace the thoughts in the minds of men that have given rise to the various words expressing death. Thus we have the Latin *mors*—allied to *moros* and *moira*, and hence, that which is allotted, appointed. But both the Hellenic and Roman mind was averse to expressing the dreadful realism of mortality, by these strong words, and sought to veil it with such circumlocutions as *vitam suam mutare*, *transire a seculo*; "Κοιμήσατο χάλκεον ὕπνον" (he slept the brazen sleep. Iliad 4th book); "τον δε σκοτος ὄσσ' ἐκάλυψεν" (and darkness covered his eyes: 6th book).

But, why should we mourn departed friends, since we know they are but lying in the *sleeping place*—*koimeterion*—'CEMETERY;' or as the vivid old Hebrew faith expressed it, *the house of the living*—Bethaim? And thus we see that Language, that primitive organic creation of the human soul, testifies to our highest intuitions and aspirations, and assures us that He who has, for a season, enveloped us in the mantle of this sleep-rounded life will again take us back to his fatherly bosom.

Thus profound are the suggestions of Words. And

even those we toss about with the most plethoric profusion and the most sacrilegious indifference are often found, when we catch the play of allusion, to be the most marvelous speaking pictures. For coming as they do from the informing mind, even the most startling metaphor and the wildest poetic image has a law and logic of its own. The Imagination bodies forth the forms of things, visionary, swift, shadowy; but the living Word—the strain or the statue or the picture, seizes the fleeting idols, and lo! they stand perennial and imperishable. Thence the Kinship of the Arts. The Arts are one in that all are outlets to the Spiritual. Beneath their finite guises gleam down glimpses of the Infinite that brightens over and embellishes all. High, clear and far up sounds their silvery voice, awaking in the vasty deeps of consciousness thrilling trembling echoes, faint and far away, of the old eternal melodies and making even

> "Our noisy years seem moments in the being
> Of the Eternal Silence!"

RAMBLE FIFTH.

FOSSIL HISTORIES

"The most familiar words and phrases are connected by imperceptible ties with the reasonings and discoveries of former men and distant times. When one counts his wealth he finds he has in his hands coins which bear the image and superscription of ancient and modern intellectual dynasties, and that in virtue of this possession acquisitions are in his power which none could ever have attained to, if it were not that the gold of truth once dug out of the mine circulates more and more widely among mankind."

WHEWELL: *Philosophy of the Inductive Sciences.*

WHAT vast historical results have come from the modern studies on Language! Comparative Philology studying languages as living organisms—subject to organic laws of growth and decay—has shown that we possess in speech a grand recorded History of Humanity, where in colossal outlines man, his affiliations, migrations, workings, growths, are drawn.

Primordial creation and manifestation of the human mind, the development of language runs parallel with the development of humanity. Language is a perfect Geology, with its strata, formations and developments, and these infinitely more intelligible than those of nature, because intellectual, and—in the sublime thought of Bunsen—carrying within themselves their order of succession in their own law of development. And what a divining-rod has language proved in the hands of the mighty modern masters! This is the true Rosetta-stone with which a Champollion and a Niebuhr and a Rawlinson have been able to set the antique nations on their feet and restore the lost threads of the genealogy of mankind. There is something sublime, and which opens up new spaces in man, in that constructive Criticism by which from slight linguistic fragments the great Niebuhr was enabled to restore the life and history of the ancient populations of Italy. And equally significant other great circles of induction. By Philologic Science the European nations have all been tracked back to Oriental fountains of wisdom and thought; Egypt has flashed up from the deeps of fifty centuries with her antique and august civilization, and now from the deciphering of the cuneiform inscriptions of West Asia are emerging those old Assyrian and Babylonian worlds, venerable with years, coevals of primeval man.

But with these colossal results of Comparative Philology it is not our present purpose to deal. What I would show is that in Words themselves we have pregnant histories embalmed—that in these medals of the mind we have the record of "ancient and modern intellectual dynasties," of vast moral and social revolutions, of the unfolding spirit of man. Words are the amber that enwraps and retains these marvelous stories, the wit and the wisdom, the fancies, the follies and the failings of humanity incarnated for ever.

Sometimes this history is that of a nation—with the Spirit of its Laws and its Religion and its Literature embalmed imperishable in these fleeting, yet immortal breathings. And often, too, these characters—these runes—are all that remain to tell the chronology of Empires perished—their

> "Cloud-capp'd towers, their gorgeous palaces,
> Their solemn temples"

all evanished, and these brief articulations alone left to tell the story of their existence. At other times the story they tell may be less important. It may be some historical event retained; some blasted hypothesis sublimated; some man immortalized; some creed with merely *verbal* credit; some poetic pulsation embodied; or, it may be a Nation's Spirit—its glory or its shame stamped in unfading colors in words that perish not. And so they all have their family secrets—with now a merely personal or incidental interest, and again of national and universal import.

And *these* are the airy, the transient utterances which we are constantly giving forth without heed, almost without a moment's reflection—tossing them from us in prodigal profusion, as if they *had* no wit or worth. Like the geodes that we find on rivers' banks which, on the outside, are rough and dirty and uninteresting, yet split them open and the cavity within holds things rich and rare—sparkling with crystals bright and beauteous. So with the words we utter. They seem from their very familiarity all trite and homely: yet beneath this conventional surface lie fine fancies, rich old legends and deep historic lore. Let us, then, in these our Rambles, like the Geologist take our (Etymologic) hammer along with us; and, laying open the rocks we may chance to meet, see if we cannot discover fossils that tell of antique worlds, and compel them to speak of the poetries and the histories and the moralities of the old Time entombed.

The term 'ROMANCE' embalms an interesting history of the chivalric era of the Middle Ages—of that epoch when, in the words of Tieck, "Believers sang of Faith; lovers of Love; knights described knightly actions and battles, and loving believing knights were their chief audience."

Fully to appreciate the origin and application of 'romance' it will be necessary to transport ourselves to France and the Ninth Century. At this period we find an important transition taking place in the language: the Latin is dying out, Frankish contributions are coming in and a new speech arising, the *Lingua Romana*—the *Romans* or *Romance* tongue. Now, as the tales of chivalry—the lays of the Troubadours and Minnesingers—so popular at this peried, were written in this idiom, the compositions themselves took the title of *Romances* (*Romans*, *romants*, *romaunts* or what not): so that, in subsequent times, any composition that partook of the nature of these songs still retained the appellation of 'romances,' and that even after the distinct class of productions to which the name legitimately belonged had died out.*

What a strange piece of history does 'ORDEAL' contain! It took its rise from a peculiar Saxon

* Bishop Percy has some interesting particulars in the third volume of the "*Reliques.*"

custom. This was the trial—*ordæl*—to which accused persons were subjected to test their guilt or innocence, and was of two kinds—by hot water and by hot iron. The modus operandi was as follows: The suspected person was forced to plunge his hand as far as the wrist, or his arm as far as the elbow (according to the magnitude of the crime) into a vessel of water boiling 'furiously hot;' take out therefrom a piece of iron of a certain weight and, after having carried it a certain distance, drop it. Then after three days the hand was inspected to see if 'foul' or 'clean'—and judgment pronounced accordingly. And this literally very 'fiery trial' it is which gives point to our 'ordeal' and perhaps lies at the root of our expression, "I would go through *fire and water* for you." *

Another social custom of the Saxons has left us several legacies. Among them every individual was valued at a certain amount of money, to which amount he was continually under bail for his good behavior. This sum, of course varied: the thane so much—the churl so much—the thrall so much: in fact it varied according to his *worth-ship*—what we now call

* For besides the ordeal by hot water there was also that of walking over red hot ploughshares. For a minute account of this curious custom consult Verstegan's "Restitution of Decayed Intelligence" and Turner's "History of the Anglo-Saxons."

'WORSHIP.' "Every man," says Sharon Turner,* "was valued at a fixed sum which was called his *were;*† and whosoever took his life was punished by having to pay this *were.*" Moreover, in addition to this, there was a pecuniary fine imposed, called the *wite:*‡ and a person thus paying the forfeiture of all his *worth-ship* presents us with the original idea of a 'FELON'—which is asserted by some to be just *feo-lun—destitute of property!* §

An interesting passage from King Alfred will give us the original form of some significant words:

"This like, O King, (*cyning*) does this present life of man on earth appear to me, compared with the time that is unknown

* History of the Anglo-Saxons, vol. II. p. 132.

† The Scotch still retain the verb "to *ware*"—that is, to expend.

‡ Compare with this the Scotch *wyte*, blame.

§ But besides having the *ware* and *wite* to pay, there was also a fine imposed for the infliction of *any* personal injury, and a curious system of anatomical economy arose. The loss of an *eye* or *leg*, for instance, was esteemed to be *worth* 50 shillings; for "breaking the mouth" a penalty of 12 shillings was imposed; for cutting off the little finger 11 sh.; for piercing the nose 9 sh.; for cutting off the thumb-nail, for the first double tooth, or for breaking a rib, each 3 sh.; for any nail and for any tooth beyond the first double tooth 1 shilling!

(*uncuth* *) to us: just like as thou sittest at feast, among thy aldermen and thanes, (*mid thinum ealdormannum and thegnum*) in winter time; and thy fire burns and thy hall is warmed. And while it rains and snows and stirs without (*and hit rene and snewe and styrine ute*), there comes a sparrow (*spearwa*), and quickly it flies through the house (*hus* †)—coming in at one door and going out at the other. Whilst it is amongst us, it feels not the wintry tempest. It enjoys the short comfort and serenity of its transient stay; but then, plunging into the winter from which it had flown, (*he roma of wintra in winter eft cymew*) it disappears from our eyes. Such is the life of man," ‡ etc.

'KING' is, we perceive, primarily *cyning* (or *kyning: cyning, cynig, cyng*=Kyng i. e. *King*), coincident with the German *König*, that is, the *can*-ning, the able, the powerful man: in regard to which hear what Verstegan tells us: "And certaine it is that the kings of monster nations were in the beginning elected and chosen by the people to raigne over them, in regard of the greatnesse of their cowrage, valour, and strength, as beeing therefore best able to defend and governe them."

'ALDERMAN' is evidently just *elderman* (*ealdorman*)

* We still say '*uncouth*' i. e. any thing that is *not couth* or *kenned*—that is *unknown* to us—a significant word indeed.

† Which we still preserve pure in *hus*band i. e. *house-bund.*

‡ Turner's Hist. Anglo-Saxons.

that is, elder-man. It has reference to the early Saxon society when the people, imagining that the *elders* would be most likely to possess wisdom and authority chose to appoint *them* as their rulers. This notion of the sagacity in grey hairs seems to have been a rather common one. Thus we have the Latin *Senatus* (our 'Senate') from *senex*, an old man; and the Greek Presbuteros—our 'Presbyterian.' Indeed Homer thus lays down the law:

> "For the minds of *young* men are ever fickle; but when a *senior* is present he looks at once to the past and the future (before and behind) that the matter may be best for both parties."
>
> *Iliad*, Book III.

> "Everich for the wisdom that he can
> Was shape lich for to ben an alderman."
>
> *Canterbury Tales.*

Chaucer does not tell us what this 'shape' *was* like; but there would seem to have been all along a fiction of it's not being very tenuous!

The very obvious connection of 'WIFE' with *web* and the verb *weave** has often been noticed: as if it

* *Wefan* is the Saxon form of the verb: German *weben*, whence 'web'; and the German *weib*—Sax. *wif*—Eng. 'wife.'

would insinuate that *weaving* is the only legitimate sphere of womanly occupation. And really I doubt we will be compelled to receive the derivation, especially since the term 'SPINSTER' appears to point in the same direction. For it is impossible to avoid perceiving that this word is formed from the verb to *spin;* and King Alfred, in his Will, designates the females of his house as the *spindle*-side. *

"My Grand father hath bequeathed his Land to the *spear-side* [or spear-*half*] and not to the *spindle-side.* If, therefore, I have bestowed any of his possessions on a female, my relations must redeem it, if they will, while she is living; but if not, it can be dealt with as we have before settled."

The Will of King Alfred, page 25.

Oxford, at the Clarendon Press, 1788.

Our industrious Saxon progenitors, therefore, took it for granted that the unmarried women would be employed in *spinning*. Chaucer makes the "Wif of Bathe" thus give us the Whole Duty of Woman:

* As the female side was designated by the *spindle*, so the male was by the *sword* or the *spear.* The Goths, however, employed a still more fantastic distinction, for man they denoted by *hat;* woman by *hood.*

"For all swiche wit yeven us in our birth;
Deceite, weping, *spinning*, God hath yeven,
To woman kindly while that they may liven."

The Wif of Bathes Tale.

Whence it would appear that there may be more than we might be apt to suppose, in the character given of a certain Roman Matron:

"Domum mansit—lanam fecit"—

so quaintly and forcibly rendered by Gawain Douglas

"She keepit close the hous, and birlit at the quhele!"

And more of this wondrous Archæology of Words. *Plagium* was among the Romans the name given to man-stealing—"the crime of knowingly buying or selling a freeman as a slave"—a species of 'plagiary' which, it would seem, by the way, is not yet quite extinct. But, since this has become less appreciable, the word is now employed to designate the more palpable *literary* thefts. Richardson cites the following:

"*Plagiarie* had not its nativity with printing; but began in times when thefts were difficult, and the paucity of books scarce wanted that invention."

Brown's Vulgar Errours.

The story which 'EMOLUMENT' tells us furnishes an additional tint wherewith to fill up the picture of primitive times: for do we not catch, lurking therein, glimpses of the *mola* or mill, far in the distance, on the edge of old Roman wood or water? And, in fact, all that 'emolument' at first implied was that *tithe of the grist* which went to the miller for grinding the grain—truly his *Emolumentum!* 'IMMOLATE' would seem to have no possible connection with the foregoing, and yet its alliance therewith is very close: *molæ* was the word used to denote grits or grains of corn coarsely ground; and, when mixed with salt, was called the *mola salsa*, or sacrifice-meal—which *mola* was sprinkled on the head of the victim previous to *immolating* him: hence its application to sacrificing, offering up. The connection of 'SALARY' with *sal*, salt is also very obvious. And in fact the *salarium* was primarily *money for salt*, then allowance of money for a journey, and then, in general, pay, allowance. It is said, moreover, that Roman soldiers were wont to receive part of their pay in salt.

The connection of 'PECUNIARY' with the primitive idea of flocks and herds (*pecus*) has already been noticed. A fragment from *Sartor Resartus*, which sounds forth here like a snatch of some antique idyl, will put the matter in its clearest light:

"A simple invention it was in the old-world Grazier—sick of lugging his slow ox about the country till he got it bartered for corn or oil—to take a piece of leather, and thereon scratch or stamp the mere Figure of an Ox (or *Pecus*); put it in his pocket, and call it *Pecunia*, Money. Yet hereby did Barter grow Sale, the leather Money is now Golden or Paper, and all miracles have been out-miracled; for there are Rothschilds and English National Debts; and whoso has sixpence is Sovereign (to the length of six pence) over all men; commands books to feed him, Philosophers to teach him, King to mount guard over him,—to the length of sixpence!"

Sartor Resartus, p. 30.

From this same root (*pecus*) we get two other instructive words, namely 'PECULIAR' and 'PECULATE.' The immediate origin of 'peculiar' is to be sought in *peculium*—"*the stock or money, which a son, with the consent of his father, or a slave, with the consent of his master, had of his own; or which a wife has independent of her husband; private property*"—hence, in general, any thing special or particular to the individual—taking away which would, doubtless, be '*peculating*.'

While on this subject it will not be amiss to cause such terms as 'wealth,' 'chattels,' 'spoil' etc. to tell us their story.

'Wealth' is evidently that which *wealeth* or maketh

a man to be *weal*, what we now call *well**—which *weal* or *well* Dryasdust makes out to mean primarily *strong*, *powerful*. Nor is this derivation at all improbable, seeing that all the purposes of wealth are originally to make one powerful, prevalent over his enemies. So 'chattel' and 'cattle' are, at first one word—(Norman catal—*katalla*); but as the principal part of their 'chattels'—their 'goods' was in the shape of oxen, sheep, etc., it is perfectly evident how the signification would become absorbed in 'cattle,' and that term be raised to typify all kinds of moveable property. One word will let us into the whole secret of 'SPOIL.' For *spolium* primarily implied *the skin of an animal stript off*, and then extended so as to embrace any 'spoils' whatsoever. A picturesque snatch of history indeed is this primitive, self-helping man—a rude Goëtz von Berlichingen—tearing from the wolf or the bear his hide and carrying it off as *spoil*. Virgil, in *Romulus*, gives us a vivid picture of the character in his old, heroic lineaments:

> "Inde lupae fulvo nutricis tegmine laetus
> Romulus excipiet gentem," etc.

* 'Weal' is now only used as a noun,

> "The *weal* or woe in thee is placed."—*Milton*.

Yet in Scotland they still use it as an adjective (*weel*).

What a long and entertaining yarn might be spun out of the '*sardonic* laugh!' We should be compelled to travel back even to the days of Greece's blind but sunny bard whom we find first alluding to the "γελως σαρδονιος." Let old, heroic Chapman recite the passage for us:

"———Who [Ulysses] he heard,
Shrunke quietly aside and let it shed
His malice on the wall. The suffering man
A *laughter raisëd most Sardonian*
With scorne, and wrath mixt."

Odyssey, Book XX.

And Richardson cites a passage from Taylor's *Pausanias* which sufficiently explains the origin and application of the term:

"This same island [*Sardinia*] is free from all kinds of poisonous and deadly herbs, excepting one herb, which resembles parsely and which, they say, causes those who eat it to die laughing. From this circumstance Homer first and others after him calls *laughing which conceals some noxious design:* 'sardonican.'"

Description of Greece, vol. iii. p. 149.

The piece of history wrapt up in 'CURFEW' is very familiar; but it will bear repetition. The composition of the word we know to be *couvre feu*, that is to say, *cover up your fires.* So that whenever

> "The *curfew* tolled the knell of parting day,"

(and the bell rang regularly at 8 o'clock every night), the good folks quietly raked up their fires, put out their lights and retired to bed, as peaceable people should do. The word reads its own story. And, by the way, it also points with unerring certainty to its originators. For we see that the word is Norman: and, in fact, this very practice was established by William the Conqueror—that grand innovator of Saxon manners and customs and introducer of French modes and morals. On this word Webster has the following curious passage: "The practice of ringing bells at nine o'clock continues in many places, and is considered, in New England, *as a signal for people to retire from company to their own abodes; and, in general, the signal is obeyed!*"

By the way, fiends and fairies, as well as mortals, were supposed to be subject to the same regulation. Thus Edgar says:

> "This is the foul fiend Flibbertigibbet: he begins at *curfew*, and walks till the first cock," etc.
>
> *Lear*, III. 4.

"RIVAL' is another word of well-known origin. The Latin adjective *rivalis* is literally that which pertains to a—*rivus*—stream or *rivu*let; and the plural *rivales* was used to designate *those who had a brook in common, or who got water from the same brook.** But, it being soon found out that this circumstance was almost constantly productive of contentions, the word lost this speciality of application, and concentrated within itself the notion of every thing that is bitter in animosity or fierce in contention. And yet Shakespeare employs the word in an altogether friendly sense. Thus when Bernardo exclaims,

> "If you do meet Horatio and Marcellus,
> The *rivals* of my watch, bid them make haste;"
>
> *Hamlet*, I. 1.

he understands and intends *partners*, *sharers*—partners in the watch, even as those who live on the same stream are sharers in the water. This use of the word is now, however, entirely obsolete. Still, we use 'COMPANION'—which may just be one who eats

* "Si inter *rivales*, id est qui per eundem rivum aquam ducunt, sit contentio de aquæ usu," etc.

Ulpian Leg. I.

(panis) *bread* along with us—in a wholly amicable application.*

The most perfect realization of the primitive conception of 'rivals' is no doubt the 'Border-men'—whom the magic wand of Sir Walter's genius has unsepulchred, causing them to spring up, clad "in complete steel," raging in the fury of their deadly feuds. We catch glimpses of the old baron issuing forth, with his troop of mailed retainers, bent on plunder, and returning with the stolen cattle of their neighbors—leaving their sign-manual in smoking houses and desolated homes.

'SIGN-MANUAL,' did we say? Even this may not be without its history. Does it not give us hints of rude lion-hearted heroes, in those rude yet romantic Middle Ages, "whose signature, a true sign-*manual*, was the stamp of their iron hands duly inked and clapt upon the parchment."†

Lo! rise there up before the mind's eye the 'CRUSADES'—those enthusiastic expeditions against the 'INFIDELS' and the 'MISCREANTS'—sending out to

* Webster, however, takes this word from *con* and *pannus*, a cloth or flag; and makes a 'companion' one who is under the same standard. He is probably right.

† Carlyle: "Stump Orator."

'SAUNTER' to the holy sepulchre whole bands of 'PILGRIMS' who came home 'PALMERS.'

In these few words lies embalmed the entire history of the movements.

The 'CRUSADES,' that is the *croisades*, or *cross*-ades—the *cross* being the banner under which they marched, each 'crusader,' moreover, bearing about with him

> "The dear remembrance of his dying Lord."

The *Holy-land*, we know, was the place whither the 'PILGRIMS' (the *pelerins*—peregrini, i.e. the *wanderers*) were wont to wend their steps; which knowing, we can readily conceive how the pilgrimage might very soon degenerate into a mere 'SAUNTERING'—and the 'PALMERS,' returning with their branches of *palm*, use this symbol only as a sanction for mendicity.

> "I am a *palmer*, as ye se,
> Which of my lyfe much part have spent,
> In many a fayre and farre countrie."
>
> *Old Play* (Quoted by Nares).

And more of the Middle Ages! Our notions of Chivalry are mainly derived from the sportive phantasy of glorious old Cervantes' 'Don Quixote;' but it must not be imagined that Miguel was the first satirist of Chivalry. Nay, our own Dan Chaucer, two hundred years before his day, has presented us with the prototype of 'Don Quixote' in his *Rime of Sire Thopas*—a stanza of which may not be unappropriate here:

> "Men speken of *romaunces* of pris,
> Of Hornchild, and of Ipotis,
> Of Bevis and Sire Guy,
> Of Sire Libeux, of Pleïndamour,
> But Sire Thopas, he bereth the flour
> Of real *chevalrie*."

'CHIVALRY' (or *chevalry*, as Chaucer more correctly writes it), we, of course, perceive to be from *chevalier* which is just a *cheval*-ier—a *horse*-man, from the fact of the knights-errant riding on horseback.*

> "Straw for Senek and straw for thy proverbs;
> I counte not a panier ful of herbes
> Of *Scole* terms."
>
> *The Merchantes Tale.*

This contempt on the part of Chaucer is doubtless justifiable enough, especially since he

* As for 'KNIGHT,' it is the Saxon *cniht*, a boy, or servant—and subsequently used to designate a youth after his admission to the privilege of bearing arms. And as this privilege was only conferred on persons of fortune or valor or favor, it acquired and retained its honorable application.

"Slept never on the Mount of Parnasso,
Ne lerned Marcus Tullius Cicero."

I quote the passage, however, merely to note the old spelling of 'SCHOOL'—*Scole*—a form which approaches nearer to the original word and gives us a glimpse thereinto. *Schole* is the etymon and signifies primitively *leisure*—the 'otium cum dignitate' so essential to permit of 'scholastic' pursuits. The following passage, cited by Richardson, well illustrates the original meaning of the word:

"For hee pictured the noble ladie Hesione, K. Alexander the Great, and Philip the King his father, with the goddesse Minerva; which tables hang in the Philosopher's *Schoole*, or *walking place*, within the stately galleries of Octavia, *where the learned clerks and gentlemen favourers of learning, were wont to meet and converse.*" *Holland's Plinie.*

The archaic use of 'CLERK,' in the above passage, suggests a remark in regard to the history of it, also.

This word has, in its transition from its original to the present application suffered divers changes in signification. Thus the word is at first one with *clergy*—(Latin *clericus*, Greek *clericos*—*cleros*)*—and

* Literally *chosen by lot*—the application of which is said by some to have originated in the choosing of Mathias recorded in the Acts of the Apostles.

then, since the clergy were supposed to absorb all the learning of the times—and what could be a more conclusive evidence of this fact than that we find 'clergie' meaning *literature?*—it came to signify a man of letters—"Every one that could read being," as Blackstone informs us, "accounted a 'clerk.'" We next find it approximating still closer to its present usage—being employed in the sense of a writer in an office: and then, by an easy gradation, a shopman, a "clerk."

We all recognize in 'FARCE' a *stuffing* of irrelevances and ludicrous conceits; but we will realize this all the more forcibly by noting that it actually does mean something *stuffed*—the verb to 'farce' being formerly used in precisely that signification, as a passage from Sir T. More will well exemplify: wherein he says with his usual causticity:

> "Which was farforth *farsed*, stuffed and swolē w^e venemous heresies."

'JEOPARDY,' again, is a word that smacks of the gaming table—the composition being in all probability that suggested by Tyrwhitt, namely, *jeu parti* —*an even game*, that is, one in which the chances are equal, so that there is a chance, and a *danger*, of its falling on either side—the whole being very *jeopar-*

dous! And this derivation wears a still more decided air of probability when viewed in connection with such passages as the following:

> "And when he, thurgh his madnesse and folie
> Hath lost his owen good thurgh *ju partie*,
> Then he exciteth other folk thereto,
> To lose his goodes as he himself hath do."
>
> *Chaucer.*

Or in the following from Froissart:

> "Si nous les voyons à *jeu partie*"—If we see them at *even game*, etc.
>
> *Chronicles*, Vol I. p. 234.

And more of the Archæology of Words!

> "The Host looked stedfastly at Adams, and after a moment's silence asked him, 'if he was not one of the writers of the *Gazetteers*, for I have hear,' says he, 'they are writ by parsons.' 'Gazetteers!' answered Adams, 'What's that?'"
>
> *Fielding's Joseph Andrews.*

Any school boy could now answer the good Parson's interrogatory; and tell him, moreover, that the 'GAZETTE' first took its name from a Venetian coin called a *gazet* or *gazetta*—and which is said to have been the price charged for perusing it. But even in England this word was used as a designation for a small coin. Thus,

> "Since you have said the word I am content,
> But will not go a *gazet* less."
>
> *Massinger's Maid of Honour*, III. 1.

A curious piece of history is contained in our application of the word 'INOCULATION.' The *application*, I say; for originally the verb to 'inoculate' merely signified to *ingraft*—literally, to insert—ocula—*eyes* i. e. buds or grafts, in a tree. And in this sense solely was it employed, until the rise of a new practice (and the necessity of a designation therefor) drew the word away from its primary usage, and gave it an application altogether novel. Here is a snatch of old rhyme-rubbish anent the subject:

> "If I had twenty children of my own,
> I would *inoculate* them every one.
> Ay, but should any of them die! what moan
> Would then be made for venturing thereupon.
> No; I should think that I had done the best,
> And be resigned whatever should befall.
> But could you really be so, quite at rest?
> I could. Then why *inoculate* at all?
>
> *Byrom on Inoculation.* (Written when first practised).

Sometimes, again, there remain to us embers and

ashes from some mighty social or political volcano, or *revolution* (which is also a turning of things upside down—*revolvo, volutum*). Instance 'SEPTEMBRIST'—a name given to those engaged in the Paris massacre of *September* '92. This same French Revolution has, moreover, left us 'SANSCULOTTES'—a term of reproach applied to the ultra Republicans—that is, fellows so wretched as to be even *destitute of breeches!* The 'CHARTIST,' too, clearly lets us know that he goes in for his *charta*, or charter: and it is perfectly evident that the 'RADICAL' believes in going down to the very *root*—radix—of the matter and upturning therefrom.

How perfectly faithful is the history 'MOB' gives us of itself. We, of course, instantly perceive it to be a shortened form of *mobile*—the variable, fickle, *mobile* crowd that is swayed about by any wind of caprice. This derivation receives an additional certificate when we learn that it was formerly written *mobile*, in full, *as a trisyllable.* Thus in the "Song of an Orange," among the *State Poems*, * we have the following:

> "Tho' the *mobile* baul
> Like the Devil and all,
> For religion, property, justice and laws."

* Vol. III. 287. In Nares' Glossary.

And in the days of Addison it was written as a contract, that is, with a dot after it. But let him speak for himself*: "It is perhaps this humour of speaking no more words than we needs must, which has so miserably curtailed some of our words, that in familiar writings and conversation they often lose all but their first syllables, as in *mob.*, red., pos., incog., and the like; and as all ridiculous words make their first entry into a language by familiar phrases, *I dare not answer for these that they will not in time be looked upon as a part of our tongue!*"

Two old Grecian words read us an instructive history. 'HYPOCRITE' and 'SYCOPHANT' namely. Let us lay open these words and see what treasures they will display. 'HYPOCRITE' is written *Hypocrites* in Greek, and in its usual application implied a *stage-player, an actor* †—hence one who feigns a part, hence a dissembler, a 'hypocrite.' But this application of the word is placed in a much clearer light when we consider for a moment certain peculiarities of the Grecian stage. From the immense extent of the ancient theatres it was necessary, in order to avoid a ludicrous disproportion, to make the players—the

* *Spectator.*

† Our verb to '*act*' is often used in the sense of feigning, pretending.

hypocrites—by artificial means, of a supernatural size. And as their rôles belonged chiefly to an antique and heroic age—'mid an atmosphere of stillness and repose—they were the more readily able to effect this. Thus they increased by a hidden trumpet, the power and volume of their voices—*and they were generally masked:* so that they were in a double and still more comprehensive and comprehensible sense, *feigners;* and our acceptation of 'HYPOCRITE' acquires from the genesis of the word increased point and pungency.

Of 'SYCOPHANT' the history is exceedingly curious. In Greece a *Sycophantes*—*sycophant*—meant a *fig-shower*—that is one who gave information of persons exporting figs from Attica, or plundering sacred fig-trees; and as such offices always carry something opprobrious with them and are eminently exposed to abuse, it soon acquired the signification of a common informer, a false accuser, a slanderer, a mean parasite. And even 'PARASITE' which I see I have just chanced to use flashes across the mind an interesting piece of history. The composition of the term would indicate that it meant originally *one who took his corn* (*sitos*) *with another*—and so lived at the other's expense. But as this privilege was, among such characters, generally paid for by obsequious flattery and buffoonery, it readily acquired the odious signification in which we now employ it.

Often, too, dwells there in some quaint old word a fund of legendary lore, at which the imagination takes flight, bearing us back to the fairy scenes of old by-gone days. 'FOXGLOVE,' for example, which is just the *folk's glove* that is, the *good folk's glove*—the 'GOOD PEOPLE' being the affectionate name by which the *fairies* were known to our simple-minded ancestors, and by which they are still designated by the Irish peasantry. We meet with the same idea in the Welsh *maneg ellyllon*—which is also the fairies' glove.

> "Delightedly dwells he 'mong fays and talismans,
> And spirits!"

'WITCH' and 'WIZARD,' too, let us into the weird phantasies of a superstitious people. For both of these words are from the Saxon verb *to know*—*wissen*—simply signifying, therefore, a *wise* person—that is, one whom *they* esteemed to be supernaturally wise.

'ROSICRUCIAN' is a word that smells of the Alchemical alembic. The composition is *ros*, dew, and *crux* (*crucis*), the cross. Now the *Rosicrucians*—those Hermetical philosophers who appeared in Germany in the Seventeenth Century—affected a know ledge of the Philosopher's Stone and other chemical arcana: so that the name is peculiarly applicable to them—*dew* being according to their notions the most powerful solvent of gold, and the *cross* being the emblem of light. Cabalistic enough!

Poor Luna, too, has had to suffer her own share of odium. Not to mention the thousand fantastic tricks formerly ascribed to her—such as her disobliging dealings with meats and men—with what infinite contempt do we talk about 'MOONSHINE;' and it is to be feared that not even advancing civilization will wholly rid us of belief in all moony influences, since we have the superstition firmly rooted in the very groundwork of our language. Witness 'LUNATIC;' also the alchemical 'MENSTRUUM' (*mensis*—a month); and, by the way, 'MONTH' itself is just the time in which it *moon*-eth.*

How often do we speak of our 'COMRADES,' and yet how seldom do we think of the allusion we continually make in doing so. The French form of this word is *camarade;* Portuguese and Spanish *camarada;* Italian *camerata.* Now this close analogy is clearly

* The steps are just these: *mooneth—moneth—month.* Chaucer will furnish examples of the middle step. Thus

"This *monethes* two."

Canterbury Tales.

significant of the common origin of these words; and in fact, we do indeed find that the root of them all is the Latin *camera*, a chamber: a 'comrade' is therefore, originally, just a *chamber-fellow*. It seems strange why the English should have corrupted this word, while in all the cognate languages it remains pure. And, indeed, we find that formerly the word was *not* 'comrade,' but *camarade*. In *Evelyn*, for instance, I find the following:

"These are the particular idioms and graceful confidences now in use; introduced, I conceive, at first by some *camerades* one with another; but is mean and rude."

Character of England.

This, indeed, is one of the most important functions of words: that they report and describe themselves, and in their simple composition, ofttimes tell us more than do the Encyclopædias. Words thus become a complete *catalogue raisonnée* of all thoughts and things; and while they are crystalized poetries and philosophies, they are at the same time important scientific organs and instruments.

The 'RUBY,' for instance, says plainly that it is *red—ruber;* and so 'RUBRIC' tells of the *red paint* with which titles of laws were first painted. The 'NEGRO' carries *black* on the very face of him, 'AUBURN' is quite literally *sun-burned* (*brennan*), while an 'ALBUM' is quite as plainly a *white tablet.* A 'RESTORATEUR' offers to *restore*, or refresh us; while an 'OMNIBUS' invitingly affirms that it is *to* or *for all;* and a 'PORTMANTEAU' jogs our memory in regard to its ability to *carry* our *mantle* for us! Then, again, 'PURGATORY' informs us that it is the place where we may *purge* out our trespasses; while 'ROSARY' proffers to conduct us through a very *bed of roses* (rosarium).

'PAPER,' again, claims an intimate kinship with the old Egyptian *papyrus;* a 'MANGER' truly tells us that it is that whereout cattle may *manger*—eat; 'LIEUTENANT' avers that he is merely one who holds the place, who stands in *lieu*, of his superior; and a 'CRAVEN' basely confesses that he has craved or *craven* his life at his enemy's hand. 'JAUNDICE' truthfully affirms that it turns its victim *yellow*—jaune; and we cannot mention 'ELECTRICITY' without being reminded of electron or *amber*—a substance which so plentifully secretes the fluid. 'AFFABLE' encouragingly assures us that it may readily be *spoken to* (affabilis); as for 'INFANT,' if it *could* speak, it would tell us that (etymologically) it *cannot* speak (in-fans).

'RECIPE' simply says, '*do thou take*' (so and so); 'RENDEZ-VOUS' says, '*betake yourselves*' (to such and such a place; and this place is the 'rendez-vous');

and the waiter when he calls, '*Anon*, sir,' means to say, '*In one* (minute), sir.' So 'BISCUIT' tells us that it is originally an article which is *bis-cuit*, *bis-coctus*—*twice-cooked;* 'SURLOIN' just informs us that it is *sur* (le) *loigne*—above the loin, although a fantastic etymology would give it the honor of knighthood and make it *Sir Loin!* A 'MINISTER' offers to *minister to*, or serve us; a 'TUTOR' offers to *look after* us (tueor) and a 'PRISON' offers to take or hold one (prendre, *pris*). 'SHABBY' affirms that it is at present *déshabillé;* while 'DANDELION' seems to claim some strange alliance with a lion's tooth—*dent de lion*, and a 'PRIVILEGE' avers that it has its own *privy*, or private *law* (lex—legis). Again, an 'AUTHOR,' if verily such, ought to be in every sense an *auctor;** that is, not merely one who produces something, but—*qui auctat*—who positively *increases* our stock of knowledge and happiness. Tried by this standard of etymology, how many of "the mob of gentlemen who write with ease," will be found wanting!

'SHROVE-TIDE' we cannot help perceiving to be the time when people were shrived, or *shriven;* so 'DEBONAIRE' is just as evidently *de bon air*—a word which has unhappily fallen into disuse, for it is both

* It was formerly so written. I have seen it thus as late as 1557.

beautiful and expressive enough to have been retained. So 'CORONER' and——so on through ten thousand other cases. But enough, enough!

The historical significance of Words springs from the fact of their being born of spontaneity. Words thus formed unwittingly, and on which the national mind, making and moulding, has wrought, must be the very expression of the national life. They are the sanctuary of the intuitions. Here we should find a people daguerreotyped in the very lineaments of life.* Nay even our common, every-day words and phrases will many a time furnish keen hints of ethnic peculiarities. Thus what is 'on the *carpet*' (*sur le tapis*) to the Frenchman, for the Englishman gets 'on the *anvil*;' nor are the 'ESPRIT' and 'CAUSERIES' of the one any more characteristic than the 'SPLEEN' and 'HUMOR' of the other; and yet the Englishman possesses a 'HOME,' while the Frenchman has only a 'CHEZ NOUS' (*at our place*). And so the Parisian's *joli* (*pretty*), to the Cockney—who is apt to cluster most of his ideas of a '*pretty* fellow' around mirth and enjoyment—becomes

* "Il est certain que la langue d'un peuple contient, s'il m'est permis de m'exprimer de la sorte, les véritables dimensions de son esprit. Il est la mesure de l'étendue de sa logique et de ses connaissances."—*M. le President de Brosses. Traité de la Formation Méchanique de Langues, etc.* Tome I. 74.

quite 'JOLLY.' And this disposition leaks out through his very amusements, so that even with his 'cards' in his hand, he will brawl and babble of 'clubs' and 'spades' (*pique et trêfle*). There is said to be no equivalent for the Italian 'CONCETTI;' while nothing could prove more mournfully the degeneracy of that once heroic people than the fact that a villain or an assassin is to them a 'BRAVO' (a *brave* man).

The coincidence of 'TRAVEL' and 'TRAVAIL' rests on a piece of history worth exploring. "Long after the Frank had achieved the conquest, he well remembered the vast amount of labor and blood it had cost him to get over the immense walls with which the Roman tried to protect his fortified encampments and towers. To scale them, to get 'trans vallum' was the most difficult part of his military labor; so he soon came, by analogy, to call every uncommon effort a 'TRAVAIL' and what the Frenchman still ascribes to the labors in childbed and the report of the Minister of Finances—apparently his hardest works as they are both called 'travail' by eminence,—the Englishman of the Middle Ages applied to his labor in travelling through foreign countries."*

It is curious, also, to note in connection with this that we always designate a literary production as a

* Prof. De Vere: Comparative Philology.

'*work*'—what the Roman termed his *opus* (plural *opera*)—what the Italian terms his *opera*, only that he, dilettante-like, applies the word exclusively to musical compositions.

In connection with 'travel' I might have noticed that what was to the Frenchman merely a *day through*, or a day's work (*journée*) became to the Englishman his 'JOURNEY'—the application of which it will not be difficult to trace.

I have spoken of our forms of greeting and parting, as 'GOOD-BYE,' which is just *God be wi' you*, 'ADIEU,' I commend you (*à dieu*) *to God*, 'FAREWELL' which is may you *fare* or *go*, well. Perhaps there is to be read in these national good wishes a deep enough lesson: perhaps it is that that these spontaneous utterances may embody the very spirit of the people. Thus the warlike Roman concentrated *his* best wishes in his 'SALVE!'—which is just 'May you be *safe*;' or into his 'VALE'—which, also, is naught other than 'May you be *well*'—following his departed friends even to the tomb with his last sad requiem,

"*Vale, vale, in eternum, vale!*"

The gay symmetrical Greek summed up his 'congratulations' in his 'χαῖρε!'—'May you be *joyful*;' while the profounder repose of the Oriental is manifested in his 'SALAAM!'—*peace!*

RAMBLE SIXTH.

WORDS OF ABUSE.

Falstaff. Away, you starveling, you elf-skin, you dried neat's tongue, you stock-fish,—O for breath to utter what is like thee! —you tailor's yard, you bow-case, you vile standing tuck:—

Prince Henry. Well, breathe awhile, and then to it again; and when thou hast tired thyself in base comparisons, hear me speak but this.

First Part of Henry IV. ii. 4.

YOU remember that the disclosure which Prince Hal makes of the merry prank played on "lean Jack" and his companions effectually closed the crater of that volcano which could vomit forth naught save wit and braggardism: otherwise we might have had a perfect exhaustion of Billingsgate from that "trunk of humors, that bolting-hutch of beastliness, that swoln parcel of dropsies, that huge bombard of sack, that stuffed cloak bag of guts, that roasted Manning-tree ox with the pudding in his belly, that reverend vice, that grey iniquity, that father ruffian, that vanity in years!"

As it is, however, we will find no lack of material wherewith to supply the hiatus. For here, at least, language is full to overflowing. It is a current which frets and foams—rushing on dashing and impetuous; which o'erleaps the barriers of custom and convention, and sweeps into its resistless torrent history and metaphor and allusion and truth and falsehood and poetry and passion and prejudice and fact and fable.

Rousseau conceived language to be the natural product of the Passions. And really the thought receives no small degree of warranty when one marks the prodigious word-fecundity of Love and Hatred—how they have ransacked heaven and earth for symbols, exhausting nature and piling hyperbole on hyperbole. Take away from any speech what these have done for it, and how small a remnant will be left! As the skeleton forms the frame-work on which the splendid drapery of the human form is placed, so the most highly elaborated speech has its roots in homely and hearty idioms and instincts—elemental utterances of human nature.

Among the most instructive of this class of words are the terms which the speech-forming faculties have loaded with burdens of abuse. A representative, that has grown familiar to us all, of this wide-spread family of words is the genus *Billingsgate*. Billingsgate pushes to enormous proportions a principle that is vital in speech. Billingsgate is the burlesque of word-building.

The metaphysics of the Abusive is exceedingly curious. The very anatomy of Passion is here exposed. Here, too, we may study elemental human nature—may read the primary thinkings and feelings of men in their first rude efforts towards expression. There are Words that remind me of the monster organisms of a primitive Geologic world. And there are workings of elemental fires visible in Language, as volcanic rocks come mounting and molten through the rib-walls of the planet.

What a subtle Analogist is Passion! It harries Nature for emblems and reads the types of humanity in bestial structures and instincts. Of the workings of this law in Words we have already met with traces. We have seen how that 'rascal' bears the primary meaning of a *mean, worthless deer*—how 'fanatic' implies a *temple-devotee*, and how 'clown' has its genesis in a tiller of the ground.

And more of these Abusive symbols.

In merrie England when the sovereign made his 'progresses' throughout the kingdom, the train of courtiers, nobles, etc., was generally followed by the attendants, and the rear brought up by the lowest class of menials—by the scullery-servants, the turn-spits, the coal-carriers and others of that ilk—rather a *black* guard, we should say: and, in fact, they were jocularly designated by this very term—an appellation which, in the shape of our 'BLACKGUARD' remains even to the present day; though why those poor devils came to be the exclusive representatives of scurrility and meanness, it might be difficult to determine—unless, indeed, as we may well suppose, they were by no means ignorant, and as little sparing in their employment, of those peculiar elegancies of diction which are playfully ascribed to that classic region where they sell the best fish and speak the best English. Burton, by the way, speaking of the various ranks and gradations of devils, alludes to this "guard:"

> "Though some of them are inferior to those of their own ranke, as the *Blacke guard* in a prince's court."
>
> *Anatomy of Melancholy*, p. 42.

From 'blackguard' we ascend to the formuling of a principle which we find exercising quite an important influence over the Abusive Element in speech, namely, that particular trades or professions or ranks in life which involve something effeminate, or mean or opprobrious—or which are supposed to do so—are taken as the types of these qualities. Thus that vile sarcasm on tailors which wickedly declares them to be but a vulgar fraction of a man is of quite dateless antiquity, while *shoemakers* are proverbially 'SNOBS.' However, we find some compensation and consolation in the fact that on this subject, too, the standards of judgment vary. In France, for instance, they do not typify this class by a shoemaker, but by a *grocer* —an 'épicier' being the very beau ideal of twopenny flash and beggarly magnificence. Another word that will conveniently come under this same category is 'FLUNKEY'—a term which, in these latter days of *flunkey-ism*, has become significant of so much, but which primarily imports merely a livery servant, a sense in which the Scotch still use it.

Of similar significance is the word 'KNAVE'—a term which has sadly lost caste—sinking down from an innocent *boy* or *youth* (as the German for boy is still *knabe*) to the very depth of rascality. The intermediate step, however, throws a ray of light on the terminus at which the word arrives. For this middle meaning is that of a *servant*—often enough, we know, apt to be *knavish*.* The course it has taken is, there-

* 'Valet' and 'varlet' were, it is surmised, originally one word.

fore, this: Primary meaning, a *youth;* secondary, a *servant;* tertiary, a '*knave.*' I shall simply exemplify under its secondary signification. Thus in the Duke of Lauderdale's (apocryphal?) translation of the Bible, the reading for, "Paul, a servant of Jesus Christ" is said to have been, "Paul, a *knave* of Jesus Christ." And in the following quaintly-curious passage from Chaucer, we have the most unequivocal proof of this employment:

"Ne tak no wif, quod he, for husbandrie,
As for to spare in houshold thy dispence:
A *trwe servant* doth more diligence
Thy good to keep, than doth thin owen wif,
For she wol claimen half part al hire lif.
And if that thou be sicke, so God me save,
Thy veray frendes or a *trwe knave*
Wol kepe thee bet than she that waiteth ay
After thy good, and hath don many a day."

The Merchantes Tale.

Deep, too, are the traces in Words of the working of the spirit of caste. 'VULGAR' properly implies what has relation to the *vulgus* or common people, as 'VULGATE' means the translation of the Scriptures made for this same *vulgus.* And it is an interesting confirmation of this thwarting of meaning that 'LEWD' which carries with it the meaning of vile, profligate, is also from a Saxon root signifying the common people—the *lay* people. So, 'MEAN' has an analogous origin witht he *many*—Saxon *mæneg;* and 'CHURL' is just the Saxon for a man, a fellow—*ceorl:** a sense which the Scotch *carle* still retains as 'cantie carle,' that is, a *merry fellow.* Again, 'BOOR' is Dutch for *farmer;* 'RUSTIC' is having relation to the *country;* 'PAGAN' is primarily a dweller in a *paganus* or hamlet; 'SAVAGE,' or *salvage* as the truer orthography would write it (Spanish *salvage,* Italian *selvaggio*), is a dweller in the *woods* (*sylva*) a *backwoodsman:* and 'VILLAIN' is primitively the serf or peasant (*villanus*) attached to the *villa* or farm. Nor does it originally bear with it any opprobrious meaning. Thus, in Chaucer:

> "But firste I praie you of your curtesie
> That ye ne asette it not my *vilanie,*
> Though that I plainly speke in this matere,
> To tellen you hir wordes and hir chere
> Ne though I speek hir wordes proprely."
>
> *Prologue to the Canterbury Tales.*

'VAGABOND,' too, is well worth exploring, being, etymologically, merely one who is given to *wandering*

* Whence Carl, Carolus, Charles, etc.

about—vagabundus—or, as we also say, 'vagrant'*—and primarily carries nothing opprobrious with it. The Prince Gonzaga di Castiglione, at least, intended to employ it in an altogether complimentary manner when, being at table with Dr. Johnson and a host of learned pundits, he called out to Johnson: "At your good health *Mr. Vagabond!*" imagining *that* to be assuredly an appropriate epithet for the author of the *Rambler!* It is curious, and not uninstructive to note in connection with this, how the *staidness* of our ancestors has stamped respectability on every thing that is *settled;* while it has cast a slight on every thing that approaches to *roving.* Thus Swift uses 'stroller' as precisely synonymous with 'vagabond;' while one given to roving is proverbially a 'ne'er-do-weel' (a *never-do-well*) as the Scotch say. Furthermore, a 'CORSAIR' (French, *corsaire;* Italian, *corsare;* Spanish, *corsario*—all from Latin curro—*cursus*, to run), is just

* Both of these words spring from one root—vagor, to *rove*, to ramble; vagabond being a corruption of *vagabundus;* and 'VAGRANT' a corruption, through the French, of the present participle. The story that these words and their analogues enwrap is curious enough. The very fact of being a *wanderer* would seem to presuppose some sinister design; and express provision is made, at least in all *civilized* countries, for the punishment of this very class. In England, for instance, the ancient punishment was, I believe, boring the ear, whipping, etc.

one who, with his vessel *runs over*, or scours the sea. 'WANTON,' too, is said to be merely one who is given to *wandering;* and there is a derivation of 'WRETCH' —in Saxon *wræcca*—which would make it out to be simply one who is *wrecked*—who is driven about and who has no certain dwelling-place!

Let me take an additional instance illustrative of this class of abusive words. It shall be 'IDIOT'—a word that has undergone some strange vicissitudes and forcibly illustrates how in Words secondary strata of signification frequently overlap the primary. The original meaning of *idiotes* is a *private person*, in contradistinction to one engaged in public affairs. Its secondary signification was one *who had no professional knowledge of any subject whatever:* and Plato makes such a collocation as this, ποιητὴς ἢ ἰδιώτης—a poet or an . . . *idiot*, by which term we are to understand a *prose-writer.* Its tertiary signification, and springing naturally out of its secondary, was that of an *ignorant, ill-informed man.*

Thus far and no farther, in Greek; thus far and no farther, in Latin. But *it never meant an 'idiot:'* that stretch of application was reserved for our modern imaginations. For even as late as the days of Wickliff, I find it employed in its legitimate signification. Thus:

"For if thou blessist in spyrit, who filleth the place of an *idyot* [qui supplet locum *idiotae*] how schal he seie amen on thi blessyng?"

I. Cor. chap. 14.

Here 'idiot' is, we know, rendered, by subsequent translations, 'he that occupieth the room of the unlearned.'

The reason of this unwarranted application of 'idiot' might be difficult to determine, unless it be that he who has not been able to get beyond the condition of a private person (ἰδιώτης) and attain to some office or honor, presents thereby prima facie evidence of not having the wit to do so and is, therefore, to be regarded as witless and imbecile!

But the Abusive faculty, not content with ransacking human nature for appellations black and bitter, is fain to go and beg or borrow from the lower animals epithets fitted to its ends. "Divers words expressive of contempt beeing," as an old English Archæologist has it, "properly the names of some vile things, and in contempt and disgrace, full often, *and with great breach of charitie*, injuriously applyed unto men and women." It is no respecter either of persons or things. Willing or unwilling, it presses universal nature into its service.

'CRONE' (whence our 'crony'), for instance, is said to be properly the appellation for a *toothless old ewe*, and then applied, in passion and sarcasm, to an old woman—an old 'hag,' which, by the way, meant primarily an enchantress or fury. 'SHREW,' also, is asserted by Lye to have been taken from the *schreawa*, or *shrew-mouse*—a little creature whose spitefulness was proverbial and whose bite and venom are even said to have been fatal.* The variations in the

* In regard to this word Webster says: "I know not the original sense of this word . . . but *beshrew*, in Chaucer is interpreted to *curse*." Most assuredly it is and quite properly, too! The fact is Webster was lead astray by Todd (see Todd's Johnson's Dict.: *in loco*) who makes the *noun* (a shrew-mouse) a derivative from the *verb* (to shrew, *to curse*). Whereas the reverse is undoubtedly the case. This arrangement, too, exhibits, and accounts for, the natural development of the derivatives. Thus:

A 'SHREW' is a woman possessed with the contentious spitefulness and venom of a shrew-mouse.

To 'SHREW' is to wish one to be struck as with the mortal venom of a shrew-mouse, and, in general, to *curse*.

'SHREWD' is just *shrew-ed*, curst, malicious—in this sense used a thousand times by Shakspeare and his cotemporaries; and then softened down to what is merely *sly, sagacious*.

To 'BESHREW' is simply another (strengthened) form of 'TO SHREW;' and hence Chaucer's 'interpretation' thereof.

orthography of 'VIXEN' will lead us, by the nearest road, up to its source: the steps are as follows: Vixen, fixen or fixin, *fox*-en = a *she-fox:* from which point of view our readers will readily perceive its peculiar applicability. And one can imagine some old hag, white and foaming with rage, endeavoring to conjure up something overwhelming wherewith to stigmatize some of her fellows—and at last screaming out, "You . . . you . . . you 'QUEAN!'" —that is, *you barren old cow—cwean* being the Saxon designation therefor.

As for 'CAT' and 'BITCH' and 'CUR' and 'HORSE' and 'ASS' and others such like, (of which we have a numerous enough tribe), they require no particularization. But it might puzzle one's wits to say what special stigmatic force there lies in 'MANDRAKE,' unless one receive all the wild fables that cluster around that strange plant.

In the following, for example, it is undoubtedly used in an abusive sense—where Falstaff, addressing his *page* says: "If the prince put thee into my service for any other reason than to set me off, why then I have no judgment. Thou whoreson *mandrake*, thou art fitter to be worn in my cap, than to wait at my heels," etc.—*Second Part of Henry IV.* I. 2.

Here, we perceive, the applicability hangs on the

old notion of the mandrake's bearing a certain resemblance to the human figure, especially to a *diminutive* person. On this quaint fancy, Nares quotes the following curious passage from Lyte: "The roote is great and white, not muche unlyke a radishe roote, divided into two or three partes, and sometimes one upon another, *almost lyke the thighes and legges of a man.*"

It was, moreover, supposed that this plant, when torn up from the ground, uttered groans so horrible as to drive any one mad who chanced to hear it.

By the way, 'MANDRAKE' is a corruption from *mandregora*—the peculiar soporific effects of which a familiar passage in Othello will have imprinted on the reader's memory:

> "———Not poppy, nor *mandragora*,
> Nor all the drowsy syrops of the world,
> Shall ever medecine thee to that sweet sleep
> Which thou ow'dst yesterday!"

Thus we often times find embalmed, even in words expressive of contempt, quite an important fact or fable. From the unpromising 'TAWDRY,' for example, we evolve quite a piece of history. For it is asserted to be a contraction from *St. Audrey* (or Saint *Ethelrida*)—a name commonly applied to an annual fair held on *St. Audrey's* day, and at which all kinds of frippery and trinkets were bought and sold: but as these articles generally possessed more *glitter* than *gold* and their splendors were too often sadly faded, it soon came to acquire the meaning which we now attach to the word 'tawdry:' '*That was bought at St. Audrey-fair!*' and so 'tawdry.' By the way, the fair saint herself is said to have been rather attached to finery—so much so, indeed, as to have died of a swelling in the throat, sent as a special visitation on account of an ardent youthful fondness for fine *necklaces!* Many of my readers may remember the very strange story which Horne Tooke compels from 'POLTROON.' He takes it from *pollice truncus*—one that has *deprived himself of his thumb*, a derivation in which he is supported by the elder Etymologists, as Vossius, Skinner and Menage. "Multi enim illo tempore, quia necessitate ad bellum cogebantur præ ignavia sibi *pollices truncabant*, ne militarent!" Some doubt has indeed been cast on this etymology and yet here is a passage giving so perfect a realization of the primary idea of 'poltroon' that one can scarcely resist accept ing it:

"In October 1795, one Samuel Caradise, who had been committed to the house of correction in Kendal, and there confined as a vagabond until put on board a King's ship, agreeable to the late Act, sent for his wife the evening before his intended departure. He was in a cell and she spoke to him through the iron door. After which he put his hand underneath, and she with a mallet and chissel, concealed for the purpose, *struck off a finger and thumb*, to render him unfit for his Majesty's service."

And similar in origin is 'SCOUNDREL'—said to be the Italian *scondaruole*, that is, a soldier who ab*sconds* or skulks at muster-*role:*

"Go, if your ancient, but ignoble blood
Has crept through *scoundrels* ever since the flood!"
Pope.

And similar, too, are 'DASTARD,' 'COWARD,' and 'CRAVEN.' A 'CRAVEN' is one who has craved or *craven* his life at his enemy's hands. 'DASTARD,' is from the Saxon verb *Dastrigan*, to be scared, frightened. And 'COWARD' is from a verb that is now obsolete in English, though it is still a living vocable in the Scotch idiom—to *cower*, to shake, to shiver. Of its use I find such examples as this:

"Winter with his rough winds and blasts causeth a lusty man and woman to *cowre* and sit by the fire."

Or this:

"And she was put, that I of talke
Ferre fro these other, up in a halke;
There lurked, and there *cowred* she."
Romaunt of the Rose.

Our slightly contemptuous term 'STICKLER' has rather an unexpected derivation. A citation from Shakespeare will let us into the secret. In *Troilus and Cressida* after

> "Achilles hath the mighty Hector slain,"

he exclaims:

> "The dragon wing of night o'erspreads the earth,
> And *stickler* like the armies separates," etc.

Like a 'stickler,' that is, like an *arbiter*. A 'stickler' in a duel was, therefore, what we now term a 'second;' and as their duty—namely that of seeing fair-play, equal advantages etc., between the combatants—would often lead them to chaffer and contend and 'stickle' in regard to special points or punctilios, we can readily conceive how it came to acquire the meaning in which it is now used. The reason of their being called '*stick*lers' is said by Stevens to have been from their carrying white *sticks* as emblems of their duty.

'HERETIC' gives us some keen hints respecting the causes of religious intolerance and the *odium theologicum*. For *Hairetikos* (Greek haireo, *to take or choose for oneself*) originally implies simply one who chooses an opinion for himself, without any reference to the truth or falsity of that opinion. But as bigotry never can endure that any man *choose* a belief that *it* does not *choose* for him and is never half so much at home as when anathemizing all who cannot subscribe *credo* to its every dogma, we can readily conceive how this innocent word acquired the meaning of one who holds erroneous and, consequently, *bad* opinions! Hobbes, in the following passage well illustrates this word:

"The word *heresy* is Greek, and signifies a *taking* of anything, particularly the taking of an opinion. After the study of Philosophy began in Greece, and the philosophers, disagreeing amongst themselves, had started many questions, not only about things natural, but also moral and civil, because every man *took* what opinion he pleased, each several opinion was called a *heresy*; which signified no more than a private opinion, without reference to truth or falsehood."

Hobbes' Historical Narration concerning Heresy.

It should also be noticed that 'INFIDEL' literally but imports one who is *faithless* (infidelis) to our beliefs. In the wars of the crusades the epithet 'infidel' was applied to the Mohammedans, even as the Normans called them 'MISCREANTS'—mescreaunts—which is also *unbelievers*. And it is a curious fact that the Turks, resenting, stigmatized the Christians as 'giaours,' which, I am told, signifies in their language *infidel* or *unbeliever*, also!

We are all familiar with what infinite contempt the Greeks were wont to look down upon all foreign nations—branding them universally as 'BARBARIANS.' The word 'barbarian' itself, however, is by no means so easily traced. Gibbon makes it Syrian, while others declare it to be merely intended as a general imitation of a (to the Greeks) foreign tongue. Thus we see how entirely relative are all such terms, whether ethical or ethnical. But so do words acquire a factitious value. How are we under the sway of Words! They tyrannize over and terrify us—

"Assume the nod,
Affect the god,"

as though they really *had* some inherent virtue and valor of their own, and were not in themselves most poverty-stricken and impotent!

In thus converting words into epithets of slight, sad injustice is often done to innocent terms. Indeed it frequently happens that words that are now employed in a scornful or opprobrious sense, were once terms of honor. Of this process of degradation 'IMP' affords a striking illustration. In Shakespeare 'imp' constantly means a *son*, and, indeed, its primary signification is a shoot or scion. Thus

"Save thy grace, king Hall, my royall Hall.
The heavens thee guard and keepe, most royall *impe* of fame."
First Part of Henry IV.

And Spenser employs it in addressing the Muses:

"Ye sacred *imps* that on Parnasso dwell,
And there the keeping have of learnings threasures."
Faerie Queene.

'BRIGAND' is most palpably formed with *malice prepense:* for originally it signified merely one who lives on a *brig*, or summit—a mountaineer. Surely the word deserves a better fate! So does 'IMPOSTER;' but, indeed, any species of *putting on* (*im-posing*) is so apt to be an *imposition* that there is no wonder the word has taken this course. But we cannot offer this excuse for a 'BELDAME'—which is every letter a *fine lady* (a *belle dame*); or, at least it is nothing worse than a *grandmother.** Chaucer furnishes examples of its employment in the first sense, and Shakespeare in the last. In the First Part of Henry IV., for instance, we find Hotspur speaking as follows:

* *Beldame* was the word for grandmother; *belsire* for grandfather. Note that a French *lady* (dame) sobers down to an English 'dame.'

"Oft the teeming Earth
Is with a kind of colic pinch'd and vex'd
By the imprisoning of unruly wind
Within her womb; which, for enlargement striving,
Shakes the old *beldame Earth*, and topples down
Steeples and moss-grown towers. At your birth
Our *grandam Earth*, having this distemprature,
In passion shook."

And why a *house-wife* or *huswife* (pronounced *huzzif* and hence the Scotch 'hizzie')—honest, thrifty soul—should degenerate into a mere 'HUSSY' seems quite inexplicable. There is surely *malice prepense* here; or else some sad degeneracy in housewives themselves! But, indeed, 'NINNY' has, if possible, received even worse usage. It is certainly so, at least, if we derive it from the Latin *nanus*, a dwarf. And as for 'NINCOMPOOP' he mournfully confesses that he is *non compos*—not of a sound mind! And yet surely 'CURMUDGEON' (*cœur mechant*, bad heart) has not so *bad a heart* as it would make us believe; while lubber, it is said, primarily implied just a tall, strapping fellow; 'JUNTO' *ought* to be nothing more than a body of men—junctus—*joined together;* a 'NATURAL' has been compelled to bear the burden of a *fool*, and 'SILLY' has its root in the German 'selig,' *blessed!*

'DOLT' is descriptive enough: it is simply one

who is *dulled*. So 'LOUT' which is connected with *low*, and 'MONSTER,' which is just a *sight*. 'RUFFIAN' is of the same root with *robber* and a 'ROUÉ' is a fellow so bad as to deserve to *be broken on the wheel!* A 'DRAB' all too truthfully declares herself to be the *drabbe*—the *lees*, or, as we say, the very *dregs* of society; while 'SCURRILITY' palpably declares that it is only fit for the mouth of a *scurra*, or buffoon. A 'CHARLATAN' (Spanish *charlar*, to prate) is quite as evidently merely a *prating* fool, and all that he says sheer 'RUBBISH' (originally something *rub*bed off, *refuse*); while a 'PETTIFOGGER' has *pettiness* or littleness written on his very face. 'CANT' is a *thing* of which unfortunately we have no lack; and yet the *word* itself is involved in considerable obscurity. However, a likely enough origin for it is the Latin *canto* (*cano*), to sing: and hence that peculiar whining, sing-song tone common to jugglers, sturdy vagabonds and other imposters religious and scientific. From the *manner* it was afterwards transferred to the *thing* itself.

Many a time, too, the Abusive reaches out to fantastic lengths. 'HAIR-BRAINED' is just *hare-brained*, a 'SCAPE-GRACE' is one who has *escaped* merely by *grace* or favor, and 'JACKANAPES' is jack and ape. So we have 'BORE,' 'BOOBY,' 'BLACKLEG,' 'BUMPKIN,'

'LOOSE-FISH,' 'SMELL-FEAST,' 'TRENCHER-FRIEND.' 'SCAMP' is connected with *scamper;* 'CAITIFF' is one who is taken—literally, *captive.* And how often do we hear persons stigmatized as 'NUMSKULLS' and 'THICKSKULLS' and 'BLOCKHEADS'—though why they should be *block*-heads, I know not; unless it be that the head of such an one may be supposed to be possessed of all the stolidity and all the *woodenness* of a *block.* As for 'RAPSCALLION,' 'SLUBBERDEGULLION,' etc., language is here whirled away into the realms of the hopelessly grotesque.

Interesting, too, are the opprobrious names that have been applied in scorn, contempt or hatred to parties and sects. The terms 'WHIG' and 'TORY,' for example, have both their origin in the malignity of the opposition. Their derivations are, however, too familiar to induce us to delay over them. However *pure* the 'PURITANS' may have been, both in walk and conversation, it did by no means save the name from falling into sad contempt; and however *methodical* the 'METHODISTS' were, it did not prevent the derision, which Sidney Smith, from the Edinburgh Review so plentifully lavished upon them, from taking effect in the scornful associations which, for so long a time, attached to the name.

In like manner, we can easily conceive how the

'QUAKERS' came to be designated by this appellation, and Dean Swift, in a passage of dubious character,* which I shall not quote, gives us the origin of the party called 'ROUNDHEADS.' In a note he says: "The fanatics, in the time of Charles I. ignorantly applying the text, 'Ye know that it is a shame for men to wear long hair,' cut theirs very short. It is said that the Queen once seeing Pym, a celebrated patriot thus cropped, enquired *who that roundhead man was*, and that from this incident, the distinction became general, and the party were called 'ROUNDHEADS.'"

Our own rich and free political life is constantly giving rise to numberless party-names of more or less interest and significance. 'HUNKER' and LOCO-FOCO' and 'FIRE-EATER' and 'DOUGHFACE' and '*Black*-republican' and the 'shells' 'HARD' and 'SOFT' and 'KNOW-NOTHING' and 'BARNBURNER' are samples, of which there are thousands, of this prodigious political activity. But as I find I shall have to devote a Ramble to the subject of Names I shall here abruptly stop.

'ROGUE' is an abusive with a double sense, being employed both in an offensive and an amiable applica-

* Tractate on "The Mechanical Operation of the Spirit."

tion—as is also the case with 'roguish:' so I shall here take occasion to make a digression on *Amiably Abusive* terms.

And how does Love bend even the most refractory words to the purposes of endearment. Every thing it conquers, and compels into its service. Under its sweet sway 'BEAR' becomes an amiable sobriquet for a husband;* nor does 'MOUSE' seem contemptible —nay, altogether endearing, as in Hamlet,

> "Pinch wanton on your cheek; call you, his *mouse*."

But Love's veritable vocabulary finds not its way into dictionaries—learned academies take no cognizance of it. The soil in which it flourisheth is by the hearth-stone and around the ingle-side. And thus do the home and hearth exercise their own sweet yet potent influence over language. They preserve it from corruption—moulding it into their own beautiful forms.

* 'Tis said that since the publication of Miss Bremer's 'Neighbours' (wherein, it will be remembered, a 'bear' figures in this way) thousands of wives have adopted this amiably abusive term. It would, of course, be impossible here to attempt entering on the subject; the vocabulary of endearment is a private one. I would merely mention the French 'BICHE,' a *hind*—which is very popular as an appellation of this sort.

A very curious and very fruitful province under the dominion of the Abusive element is Oaths. Of cursing and swearing—that senseless and sinful practice—we speak not; but of those more innocent, yet characteristic *exclamations* and other popular and peculiar idioms and phrases by which we often contrive to communicate thoughts and fancies and feelings which it would be impossible otherwise to convey. Thus I know of no equivalent for the common exclamation 'The Deuce!' It bears with it a burden of significance not its own and which no other term can fitly represent. By the way, this word is said to be the Gallic name of a demon or evil spirit. Augustine, in his *City of God*, mentions the word:

> "Quosdam dæmones quos *dusios* Galli nuncupant."

An emotion there is, which only '*whew!*' can perfectly symbolize: and so with a thousand lights and shades of meaning, which only such interjectional articulations can fully convey. Indeed we should say that some of the keenest instruments and organs of thought had not yet found their way into words. The 'DICKENS!' for instance, which is said to be just the 'deil!' and——but 'tis needless to enumerate.

* See Webster.

I shall not enter into the dark abyss of terms formed by that disgraceful practice of swearing: it is curious, however, to note the characteristic oaths of different nations. Thus the Frenchman swears 'Par bleu' and by his 'mille tonnères!' while the German growls out his 'Donner und Blitzen!' or 'Donner und Teufel!' as Jean Paul often has it.

So we see that oaths are not only national, but individual. Thus how famous is Socrates' 'By the dog!' And Charles' 'Odd's death!' Just as notorious, however, is the 'God's death!' of good Queen Bess. Swearing, indeed, Elizabeth affected as she did many other manly accomplishments. For if she could sing 'ditties,'

"———In a summer's bower,
With ravishing division to her lute;"

she was also quite as able, when occasion required, heartily to cuff her courtiers. It would seem, however, that ladies once enjoyed a much larger share of this peculiar prerogative than at present. We should, at least, conclude so from Hotspur's exhortation to his wife:

"*Hotspur.* Come, Kate, I'll hear your song, too.
Lady Percy. Not mine, *in good sooth.*

Hotspur. Not yours, *in good sooth!* 'Heart, you swear like a comfit-maker's wife! Not you, *in good sooth;* and, *As true as I live;* and, *As God shall mend me;* and, *As sure as day;*

And giv'st such sarcenet surety for thy oaths,
As if thou never walk'dst further than Finsbury.
Swear me, Kate, *like a lady* (!), as thou art,
A good mouth-filling oath; and leave *in sooth,*
And such protests of pepper-gingerbread,
To velvet guards and Sunday citizens!"

First Part of Henry IV. III. 2.

'ZOUNDS!' is a common enough exclamation, and is probably a contraction for *God's wounds*—a form which we find in Chaucer, who is overflowing with quaint asseverations of this kind. Thus we find,

"I make a vow by *Goddes digne bones.*"

The Pardoneres Tale.

'PERDY,' again, is just a corruption for *par dieu* (by God). So, 'GRAMERCY' returns—*grand merci*—great thanks. Of this primitive form Chaucer will afford us an example:

" *Grand mercy,* lord, God thank it you (quod she)
That ye have saved me my children dere."

The Clerkes Tale.

'BY'R LADY,' that is *by our lady* (the Virgin Mary),

and 'BY'R LAKIN'—that is, *by our ladykin*—a diminutive of the preceding—were once (when 'our lady' received more veneration than she now does) very popular forms of asseveration. So Snout the tinker, exclaims:

> "*By'r lakin*, a parlous fear!"
> *Mid Summers Night's* Dream, III. 1.

Falstaff, on the contrary, is constantly swearing 'BY THE LORD!' and declaring (what he certainly well merited) 'I'LL BE HANGED!' Whereas Justice Shallow prefers to point his declaration 'BY YEA AND NAY,' or 'BY COCK AND PYE' (a corruption for *God and Pye*—the latter being the name given to the Popish book of church offices—By God and the Book!) Another whimsical form of swearing was 'By these ten bones!' i. e. the *fingers* or 'by these pickers and stealers' (Hamlet). See Shakespeare, Jonson, etc.

We of the Saxon brood are perhaps as abusive in our language and as terrible in our oaths as any nation on the face of the earth. So much so, that we can scarcely tax Caliban with extravagance when he declares:

> "You taught me language, and my profit on't

Is, I know how to curse; the red plague rid ye
For learning me your language."*

Tempest.

It is averred, indeed, that the Italians outstrip us in this matter, as in many other arts—worthy and unworthy; but this is to be regarded as dubious!

We have seen how Shakespeare wields this class of words—conjuring up the most fantastic or ludicrous or scurrilous combinations—piling term on term and capping the climax of the ridiculous or the abusive. Like a Titan, he laughs and sports amid the spoils of language—playing with and tossing about words—or rattling them like a tempest of hail stones about the ears of some luckless wight.

"Ha, thou *mountain-foreigner!* Sir John, and master mine,
I combat challenge of this *latten bilbo;*
Word of denial, *froth and scum*, thou liest."

Merry Wives of Windsor, I. 1.

"Out of my doors, you *witch*, you *hag*, you *baggage*, you *pole-cat*, you *ronyon.*"

Ibid, IV. 2.

* Caliban imprecates the 'red plague.' The names of frightful diseases are often used as imprecations. Thus, the old 'Pox on you!' was, previous to the introduction of vaccination, a fearful curse. Thank vaccination, then, for removing both the thing and the word!

So with a 'murrain!' etc., etc.

"Get you gone, you *dwarf;*
You *minimus*, of *hind'ring knot-grass made;*
You *bead*, you *acorn*."

Mid-Summer Nights' Dream, III. 2.

"*Falstaff.* Strike; down with them; cut the *villains'* throats, oh! *whoreson caterpillars! bacon-fed knaves!* they hate us youth; down with them; fleece them.

Hang ye *gorbellied knaves;* are ye undone? No, ye *fat chuffs;* I would your store were here! On, *bacons*, on! What, ye *knaves*, etc."

First Part of Henry IV. II. 2.

However, Falstaff many a time gets paid back in his own coin:

"You will, *chops?*

Farewell, thou *latter-spring!* Farewell, *all-hallown summer!*

Peace, ye *fat-kidney'd rascal!* . . . Peace, ye *fat guts!*

Call in *ribs*, call in *tallow*.

Here comes *lean Jack*, here comes *bare-bone!*"

And so we leave off, even as we began:

"Why, thou clay-brained guts; thou knotty-pated fool; thou whoreson, obscene, greasy, tallow-keech ———!"

RAMBLE SEVENTH.

FANCIES AND FANTASTICS.

"The same old love of laughing in this beautiful mad-house of Earth."

JEAN PAUL RICHTER.

MOTLEY ever are the minglings of this strange, sleep-rounded life,

"A wedding or a festival,
A mourning or a funeral."

And Speech reflects this infinite richness and variety. For if language has run pliant and plastic into the mould of our every-day thoughts and feelings, lending itself to the uses of the Understanding and the Common Sense, and smacking of our workshop world, yet can it also

"Babble of green fields."

If it generally exhibits but broad high-ways and level plains—*platitudes* often enough: yet does it many a time lead off through by-paths to wild woods and cavernous depths and elfin haunts, where visionary forms and rustling spirit-voices meet eye and ear!

The Grotesque and Arabesque play through speech. Children of the nimble fancy, they round our language with a fringe of smiles and tears. The fantastic in Words is but a reflection of the fantastic in Things. For Nature, too, loves a freak. And as, amid the infinite variety of organic and inorganic forms, creative energy at times sports in seemingly lawless prodigality, so the informing Fancy has interwoven in words its fairy imaginings—

> "Retinues of airy kings,
> Skirts of angels, starry wings!"

'NIGHT-MARE' is a snatch of fancy taken from the Scandinavian mythology. In that mythology *Mara* was a Finland elf, who in *night*-sleep came with horrid visitation to men. And in Laing's Chronicles I find as follows:

"Vailand who ruled over the Upsal domain, was bewitched by the elf Mara. He became drowsy, and laid himself down to sleep; but when he had slept but a little while, he cried out, saying, Mara was treading on him; but when they took hold of his head she trod upon his legs, and when they laid hold of his legs, she pressed upon his head and it was his death."

Chronicles of the Kings of Norway.

'PREPOSTEROUS' is curious enough. It is *præ* and *posterus*, having that *before* which ought to come *after*—"putting the cart before the horse," as we say; and how could one be more perfectly brought to a stand than by being 'non-plussed'—that is, so bamboozled as to be able to say—non plus—*no more!* 'INTERLARD' is plainly the mixing *fat and lean*—entrelarder; to get things 'on tick' is properly to get them *on ticket* or bill—a form common in old literature; a 'HABERDASHER' has, according to Minsheu, a fantastic genesis in the expression of a shopkeeper offering his wares, *Habt ihr dass?*—*have you this;* 'TEETOTALISM' is just T-totalism, that is *temperance-totalism!* and 'NEWS' is matter brought from all quarters—(N)orth, (E)ast, (W)est, (S)outh = N E W S!

But these Gypsies of language, seemingly so destitute of history or ancestry, do often, when keenly tracked, reveal long historic processes in their composition. What a strangely extravagant round has the word 'LOCO-FOCO' taken! We first have it, probably as a corruption of *loco foci* (i. e. *in place of a fire*) and so applied to lucifer matches (*lucifer* matches! that is, *light bringing* matches)—and then by a bizarre incident, in which lucifer matches acted a part, applied as a designation of a particular political party. The occasion of its application is said to have been as follows. At a meeting of the extreme democrats in Tammany Hall, New York, there was a great diversity of opinion, and consequently great confusion—on account of which the chairman left his seat and the lights were extinguished with a view to dissolving the meeting; when those in favor of extreme measures produced *loco-foco* matches, rekindled the lights, continued the meeting, and accomplished their object. Hence the name of 'LOCO-FOCO' which continueth even unto this day. Again, the familiar phrase to 'OUT-HEROD HEROD,' is not a mere chance-combination, but holds in itself the pith and marrow of a thousand legends. In regard to King Herod we are merely told that "he sat upon a throne and made an oration" unto the people—of what character we are not informed, and yet from subsequent events and the awful punishment which befel him, we may reasonably conclude that it was bombastic, bold and blasphemous. But in the old 'Mysteries' and 'Moralities' he is constantly represented as of a fierce, proud, virulent character. Now it was doubtless from these that Shakespeare drew the expression: and hence its peculiarly expressive power.

That old expression to sit 'above, or below the salt' becomes instinct with meaning when we recollect that it was the custom, in old times, to place a large dish of salt about the middle of the table, 'above' which the more honorable guests were wont to sit, while the vulgar took their places in unnoticed obscurity 'below.' And Sidney Smith thus gives us the origin of the expression 'within or without the pale:' "The limit which divided the possessions of the English settlers [in Ireland] from those of the native Irish was called the *pale;* and the expression of inhabitants *within the pale* and *without the pale*, were the terms by which the two nations were distinguished."*

The phrase 'I don't care a fig' would seem, at the first blush, to contain no special force, the *fig* being to us rather a valuable article;† but the expression rises to pungent point when we recollect that the phrase is an importation from the Spanish, *figo* or *fico* being in that language an obscene expression, as in Shakespeare:

> "*Pistol.* Die and be damned; and *figo* for thy friendship!
> *Fluellen.* It is well.
> *Pistol. The fig of Spain!*
> *Fluellen.* Very good." *Henry V.* III. 6.

* Edinburgh Review: article on "Parnell and Ireland."

† Our 'Not a straw'—what the Latins named *nihil* (ne hilum)—would seem to carry more force.

Certain words, indeed, are absurdly fantastic, mere *lusus verborum:* and it is only their history, that comes in to integrate them with by-gone circumstances, that can restore them to the region of common-sense. For example, five important sea-port towns, on the eastern coast of England, opposite France, were properly enough called collectively the *Cinque-ports*, or *five harbors;* but, when, forgetting the literal import, people came to speak about *seven* of the 'Cinque-ports,' it assuredly became more than most ridiculous. 'DEAN' (*decanus*) is properly the leader of a file *ten* feet deep. 'QUARANTINE,' again, we plainly perceive, implies the *forty* days during which ships suspected of carrying disease were obliged to wait; but such combinations as a 'quarantine' of *five*, or of *ten* days twist arithmetic out of all proportion. To be sure, it will not do for us to make any violent protest against the like anomalies, as this overlaying of primary by secondary formations is fundamental in the philosophy of Speech: but the process none the less demands vigilant oversight.

Then, there are pure pieces of whimsey. 'KICKSHAW' is an instance to the point—supposed to be intended for 'quelque chose,' that is, *something*, and hence quite suitable for aught "fantastical, uncommon, or that has no particular name," as the dictionaries define it. As for 'QUANDARY,' that is still worse:

> "*Falstaff.* Mistress Ford;—come, Mistress Ford,—
>
> *Quickly.* Marry, this is the short and the long of it; you have brought her into such a *canaries* as 'tis wonderful. The best courtier of them all, when the court lay at Windsor, could never have brought her into such a *canary.*"
>
> *Merry Wives of Windsor*, II. 2.

And into a pretty 'canaries,' too, has good Mistress Quickly brought her words! For the term she intended is, at its best, 'quandary,' and that is fantastic enough—being, as is supposed, a corruption for *Qu'en dira-t-on—What will they say?*—which, though not very elegant, is yet sufficiently descriptive of being in a terrible *fix!*

A few Latin whimsicalities may not be out of place here. 'Hocus pocus' is one of the most outré of the tribe, and has a fantastic enough origin. Fantastic, at least, if we make it a corruption of *Hoc est corpus* (Christi); if it be true that the ignorant and juggling 'priests' "who gabble Latin which they do not understand," instead of saying *Hoc est corpus meum* transformed it into *hocus pocus* (*meum*)!* May we not

* There are, of course innumerable etymologies for this phrase: Some (Todd, Johnson's Editor, among them) take it

legitimately enough form 'HOAX' from this? To *hocus*, indeed, I find originally used in the same sense. Henry VII. is said to have told a story similar to this, of a stupid old monk who, in repeating his breviary constantly put *mumpsimus* instead of *sumpsimus;* and who, on being told of his mistake said it might be so for what he knew, but "*mumpsimus* was what he was taught and he would continue to say it"*—hence 'mumpsimus,' though discarded now, was formerly used for an ignorant and incorrigible blunder. Ignoramuses all of them! And yet 'IGNORAMUS' itself is extravagant enough: for it is evidently the first person plural of the present indicative of the verb *ignoro*, i.e., *we are ignorant*—and, according to Webster, "the

from *Ochus Bochus*, the name of a famous magician which the Italian conjurors were wont to invoke. Webster says it is *Welsh!*—but we have no patience to quote the trash. *Risum teneas!*

In regard to the above derivation Pegge says: "This we may believe when we are told that they [the priests] call part of the funeral service, *De Profundis*, by the style and title of *Deborah Fundish:* after which we cannot be surprised that an ignorant imprisoned Cockney pick pocket should call a *Habeas Corpus*—a *hap'oth of Copperas*, said to be the language of Newgate."

Pegge's Anecdotes of the English Language, p. 75.

* Nares' Glossary.

indorsement which a grand jury make on a bill presented to them for inquiry, when there is not evidence to support the charges!" The word deserves a better fate.

We all remember Hudibrastic Butler's lines on that Scholastic limbo

> "Where *Entity* and quidity
> The ghosts of defunct bodies fly."

Most assuredly *defunct*—with very little *somethingness* (to render *quiditas* literally) left; except that the lawyer has inherited the 'quiddits' and the 'quillets.' Of their 'QUODLIBETS,' the elder D'Israeli thus discourses: "The Scholastic questions were called *Questiones Quod libeticæ;* and they were frequently so ridiculous that we have retained the word *Quodlibet* in our vernacular style to express anything ridiculously subtile; something which comes at length to be distinguished

> 'With all the rash dexterity of wit.'"

But we have not done with our Latinisms yet. Thus have we not still 'QUORUMS:' that is to say, bodies—quorum—*of whom* these present are legally sufficient to transact the business. 'QUIDNUNCS' are at present quite as anxious as ever to know *what now?* while there would seem to be even an increase of ignorant empirics, with their 'NOSTRUMS,' in regard to which they vauntingly say: "Id *nostrum* est—this is *ours*—an arcanum which nobody else possesses, and wherewith we will cure all your maladies!" From quacks and quackeries we naturally stroll to 'MOUNTEBANKS'—who, it is evident, have their character lurking out from their very name: for it is impossible to conceal from us, that he is just one who *mounts the bench* (monte banc), and there rants respecting his own skill and the infallibility of his medicines; often, however, managing very effectually to 'gull' and 'coney-catch' (what very *rabbits* they must be) the 'greenhorns'—*literally* such.

Talking about 'gulling' (which we still have) and 'coney-catching' (which we do not have), I should notice that D'Israeli, in the "Curiosities of Literature," has a curious passage in regard to this practice, which the reader may consult for himself.* And in Overbury's *Characters*, we have also the following:

"He cheats young *guls* that are newly come to towne; and when the keeper of the Ordinary blames him for it, he answers him in his owne profession, that a *woodcocke* must be plucked ere it be drest."

* Page 230 and following.

The allusion to the *woodcock* as typical of a person of intense verdancy and witlessness was quite in vogue some time ago. Thus we have in Shakespeare:

> "O this *woodcock!* what an ass it is!"
>
> *Taming of the Shrew*, I. 2.

See, however, when we think of it for a moment, what a curious collocation is thus produced—a *wood cock* and an *ass!* But so has language in its hot pursuit of analogy harried creation for emblems. A modern poetical anatomist has thrown out the intimation that the whole animal kingdom is simply man disintegrated. And assuredly we have in language a record of how the apprehensive fancy has seized on animal suggestions as symbols of metaphysical and moral qualities. Thus we typify courage by the 'lion;' ferocity by the 'tiger' (wolf, etc.); frolicsome gentleness by the 'lamb'—provided, indeed, this amiable quality degenerate not into '*sheep*ishness;' and '*beast*liness' in general by the hog! How keenly do we characterize, when we speak about a boy 'playing fox;' or of one '*crow*ing' over another, or of a woman '*gad*-ding' about! So, too, our 'BUCKS' —I fear they almost deserve the name of 'COXCOMBS' (i.e. *cock's combs*),—often enough go out a-'*lark*ing,' and '*caper*ing' about (*caper*, a goat)—which is very much like a *goat*, indeed!

And more from the animal world. The ichthyologic fact of the *gudgeon's* easily swallowing the bait has been imported by the vivid fancy into speech in the word 'GUDGEON'—a term expressive of a facile disposition with whom anything readily *goes down.* Cicero traces a curiously fantastic connection between 'MUSCLE' (*musculus*) and *musculus*, a little mouse; and the *raven* has got itself into language in our '*ravenous*.' The Etymologists charge the *cuckoo* with having fathered that ugly word 'CUCKOLD' upon us;* while 'COWARD' is asserted by the old lexicographs to be just a contraction for *cow*-hearted—a derivation which certainly does not stand any very close test, though it is not without a degree of vraisemblance when we view it in connection with our verbs to *cow*, *cower* etc.† So our verb to 'HAWK'

* But see Tooke's "Diversions of Purley," under this word: and for the connection of the Scotch 'GOWK' therewith, see Jamieson's Scottish Dictionary.

† If, as is asserted, the original French orthography of 'coward' were *culvert*, the derivation, which has been proposed, from *culum* and *vertere*—*to turn the tail* (very 'coward' like, indeed!) will receive countenance. See Minshew and Menage; also Tooke, and Tyrwhitt on Chaucer.

and the substantive 'HAWKER' may possibly have reference to one who carried round *hawks* for sale. Moreover the wooden frame in which he kept his birds he called a 'CADGE' whence we have the old English (and the present Scotch) 'CADGER' which in English becomes a very queer 'CODGER!'

But can the grotesque of animal symbolism farther go than in those curiously complicated allusions to *rats* and *rhyming* which we find scattered throughout the elder dramatists. Thus in *As You Like It*, Rosalind says, apropos of the profusion of verses lavished on her:

"I was never so be-rhymed since Pythagoras' time, *that I was an Irish rat*, which I can hardly remember."

And you may remember the very sarcastic witticism which Dean Swift, in his *Advice to a Young Poet*, picks out of it:

'Sir Philip Sidney," observes he, "mentions *rhyming to death*, which is said to be done in Ireland; and truly, to our honour be it spoken, that power, in a great measure, *continues with us to this day!*"

But anent *rats and rhyming*, let old Verstegan tell us a story that will set the matter in its clearest light:

"There came into the town of *Hamel* in the countrey of

Brunswyc an od kynd of compagnion, who for the fantastical cote which hee wore beeing wrought with sundry colours, was called the pyed pyper; for a pyper hee was besydes his other qualities. This fellow forsooth offred the townsmen for a certain somme of mony to rid the town of all the rattes that were in it (for at that tyme the burgers were with that vermin greatly annoyed). The accord in fyne beeing made; the pyed pyper with a shril pype went pyping through the streets, and foorthwith the rattes came all running out of the houses in great numbers after him; all which hee led unto the river of *Weaser* and therein drowned them. This donne, and no one rat more perceaved to bee left in the town; he afterward came to demaund his reward according to his bargain, but beeing told that the bargain was not made with him in good earnest, to wit with an opinion that even hee could bee able to do such a feat; they cared not what they accorded unto, when they imagyned it could never bee deserved, and so never to be demaunded: but nevertheless seeing hee had donne such an unlykely thing in deed, they were content to give a good reward; and so offred him far less than hee lookt for; but hee therewith discontented, said he would have his ful recompence according to his bargain, but they utterly denying to give it him, hee threatened thē with revēge; they bad him do his worst, whereupon he betakes him again to his pype, and going through the streets as before, was followed of a number of boyes out at one of the gates of the citie, and coming to a little hil, there opened in the syde thereof a wyde hole, into the which himself and all the children beeing in number one hundred and thirtie did enter; and beeing entred the hil closed up again, and became as before.

A boy that beeing lame and came somewhat lagging behynd the rest, seeing this that hapned returned presently back and told what hee had seen; foorthwith began great lamentation among the parents for their children, and men were sent out with all dilligence, both by land and by water to enquyre yf ought could bee heard of them, but with all the enquyrie they could possibly use, nothing more than is aforesaid could of them be understood. In memorie thereof it was then ordayned, that from thence-forth no drum, pype or other instrument, should be sounded in the street leading to the gate through which they passed; nor no osterie to bee there holden. And it was also established, that from that tyme forward in all publyke wrytings that should bee made in that town, after the date therein set down of the yeare of our Lord, the date of the yeare of this going foorth of their children should bee added, the which they have accordingly ever since continued. And this great wonder hapned on the 22. day of Iuly, in the yeare of our Lord one thowsand three hundreth seaventie, and six."

Restitution of Decayed Intelligence, 85.

Big words! Here, too, the grotesque comes into play. And what a subtle psychology lies in these Cyclopean efforts of the human mind. The affectation of words *big* merely for the sake of their *bigness* is limited to no country and to no age. 'SLUBBERDEGULLION,' which Butler employs in Hudibras, affords an example to the point. So also 'SPLENDIDIOUS' used by Drayton, though without the sanction either of etymology or analogy. Shakespeare is in these extravaganzas, as everywhere, pre-eminent. Instance his 'ANTHROPOPHAGINIAN' which the Host, in The Merry Wives of Windsor, gets off in order to overwhelm poor Simple:

Host. What wouldst thou have, boor? What, thick-skin? Speak, breathe, discuss; brief, short, quick, snap.

Simple. Marry, sir, I come to speak with Sir John Falstaff, from Master Slender.

Host. There's his chamber, his house, his castle, his standing-bed and truckle-bed; 'tis painted about with the story of the prodigal, fresh and new; Go, knock and call; he'll speak like an *anthropophaginian* unto thee: knock, I say.

Merry Wives of Windsor, IV. 5.

In the days of good Queen Bess, while through the brain of "Sweet Will" Tempests and Mid Summer Night's Dreams were singing themselves, lived also one John Lylly who became the founder of a new *Ism* —*Euphuism*,* namely, or Fine Speaking—a species of bizarrerie which, by the constant use of the farthest-fetched allegory and the most farcical bombast, succeeded in producing some of the most extraordi-

* His two books are entitled, "Euphues and his England," and "The Anatomy of Wit." Sir Walter Scott, it will be remembered has, in the "Monastery," a popular representation of Euphuism in the character of Sir Percie Shafton.

nary contortions of which our language could be imagined susceptible. Immense, however, was the success of the Euphuist. Indeed it was for a time pushed to perfect mania. "All our ladies," says Blount, "were then his scollers, and that beautie in Court who could not *parley Euphuesme* was as little regarded as shee which now there speaks not French." Blount was the Editor of Lylly's books, and, of course, an adoring admirer of him: and as the panegyrics he pronounces on his master are altogether in the Euphuistic style I shall quote one of them: "The witty, comical, facetiously quick, and quickly facetious John Lylly—he that sat at Apollo's table and to whom Phœbus gave a wreath of his own bays without snatching!"

Shakespeare's keen eye, however, soon penetrated the affectation, and accordingly we find him taking frequent occasion to ridicule the absurdity. Thus in the First Part of Henry IV., and also in the character of Osric, in Hamlet, we have a perfect characterizing of the Euphuistic courtier of his day. Hamlet's summing up of the character is so complete that I really cannot resist quoting it:

"He did comply [i.e. *compliment*] with his dug, before he sucked it. Thus has he (and many more of the same breed.

that, I know, the drowsy age dotes on) only got the tune of the time and outward habit of encounter; *a kind of yesty collection, which carries them through and through the most fond and winnowed opinions; and do but blow them to their trial, the bubbles are out.*"

Hamlet, V. 2.

Euphuism died a natural death. Its ghost has, nevertheless, appeared at various periods, in various guises. Often, indeed, in the shape of a most abominable affectation of Gallicisms—of which take but one example:

"I was *chez moi*, inhaling the *odeur musquée* of my scented *boudoir*, when the Prince de Z. entered. He found me in my *demi-toilette*, *blasée surtout* and pensively engaged in solitary conjugation of the verb *s'ennuyer;* and though he had never been one of my *habitués*, or by any means *des nôtres*, I was not disinclined, at this moment of my *delassement*, to glide with him into the *crocchio restretto* of familiar chat!"

*Lady Morgan's New Monthly.**

So much for a class of writers of which literature has never been destitute of specimens, and in reference to whom we can most heartily say, with Mercutio:

* The later productions of Madame D'Arbly are replete with illustrations.

"The pox of such antic, lisping, affecting fantasticals; these new tuners of accents!—*By Jesu, a very good blade!—a very tall man!*—Why, is not this a lamentable thing, grandsire, that we should be thus afflicted with these strange flies, these fashion-mongers, these *pardonez mois*, who stand so much on the new form, that they cannot sit at ease on the old bench? O, their *bons*, their *bons!*"

Romeo and Juliet, II 4.

Sometimes, indeed, we proceed to the opposite extreme and clip our terms so villainously short—so curtail them—that they are scarcely recognizable. Such are some already noticed, as *Mob.*, *Red.*, *Incog.* —Such also are *Do.*, *Pro* and *Con.*, and the old *obs.* and *sols.* (contracted from *objectiones et solutiones*). 'PUG' and 'NUNCLE' are additional examples. So, too, *Have or have not* shortens into '*Hob or nob*;' *To Do off or do on* (i.e. to put off, or put on) appears in the guise of to '*Doff or don*,' and *cousin* very soon becomes sweet 'COZ.'

Diminutives, indeed, are the natural language of love: a principle which could receive no more forcible illustration than the abbreviations of proper names. This is constantly done by familiarity and friendship. A monosyllable—which the popular instinct always struggles towards—is warm and cozy—hearty as the pressure of a friend's hand; a polysyllable is stiff and formal—suspicious as the obsequious bow of a courtier. 'Frank' and 'Ben' and 'Will' are seated at the heart's hearth-stone, while *Malachia*, *Obediah* or *Jeremiah* are knocking, unheeded at the door.

Nares quotes a curious passage on this subject from Heywood, a few lines of which may be worth citing. Talking of the old poets—his contemporaries—he says:

> "Excellent *Bewmont* in the foremost ranke
> Of the rar'st wits, was never more than *Frank.*
> Mellefluous *Shakespeare*, whose inchanting quill
> Commanded mirth or passion, was but *Will.*
> And famous *Jonson*, though his learned pen
> Be dipt in Castaly, is still but *Ben.*
> *Fletcher* and *Webster*, of that learned packe
> None of the mean'st, yet neither was but *Jacke*
> *Decker's* but *Tom*, nor May nor Middleton.
> And hee's now but *Jacke Foord*, that once was John!"
>
> *Hierarchie of Blessed Angels, B.* 4.

De Quincy I think it is who exhibits this same principle of abbreviation applied to the classic writers. Thus *Quintus Horatius Flaccus*, is, with us, just that jolly dog *Horace; Publius Virgilius Maro* has dwindled down to the familiar *Virgil* and *Caius Crispus Sallustius* glories in the simple sobriquet of *Sallust.* It is curious, also, to observe, in this connection, the names which have *not* been shortened, and to trace the cause thereof—whether from the writer's not being naturalized in the country, or what not. But so much for names.

We might discover, to push the matter of abbreviations a little farther, something fantastic even in particular letters. That learned man Jovianus Pontanus writ two books concerning that strange rune 'H;' 'S' has a long and mystic history. Not to mention the cabalistic use made of the *Runes*, and the *semi-sacred* letters of the Hebrews, how contemptuously do we talk about persons who are not able to tell a 'B from a Bull's foot;' while 'R' was, we know, long called the *dog's letter*—an instance of which we have in the dialogue between the Nurse and Romeo, in *Romeo and Juliet:*

> *Nurse.* Doth not Rosemary and Romeo begin both with a letter?
>
> *Rom.* Ay, nurse; what of that? both begin with an *R.*
>
> *Nurse.* Ah mocker! that's the dog's name; *R* is for the dog. No: I know it begins with some other letter, etc.
>
> *Romeo and Juliet,* II. 4

The mention of 'rosemary,' by the nurse, in the above passage, suggests a remark thereanent. Note, however, that it has no connection whatever with

Rose-Mary as, at first sight, one might be apt to suppose; but is simply a corruption for *ros marinus*—the sea-rose. Such hybridisms are, yet, by no means uncommon in our language, nor are they confined to any particular language. The principle in their formation seems to be just this: when a foreign word makes its appearance, the *people*—who are ever (spite of Dictionaries and Philologic Academies) the real language-makers—immediately attempt to bend it to some familiar form—to give it

"A local habitation and a name"

among them. Nor is it to be wondered at, if oddities and whimsicalities are often enough the result. Thus the French *Cartreuse* has transformed itself into our '*Charter-house*;' the German *vertugale* we are fain to turn to some account, and so we make it a '*farthingale*;' while the Roman *Asparagus* springs up in British soil, as '*sparrow-grass*,' and 'STAVES-ACRE' (a medicinal plant)—a word formerly in use—is just a corruption of the Greek σταφις αγρια!*

* I might have noticed, before leaving this subject, the very curious shapes, which the names of European taverns often assume. Thus the 'BACCHANALS' has become the 'BAG AND NAILS,' while 'BOULOGNE MOUTH' appears as the 'BULL AND MOUTH' etc. See, also, De Vere's *Comparative Philology*.

Often times there would seem to be some strange fatality attached to certain words. For we see them wafted by favoring gales to the very zenith of popularity—swaying and registering the sentiment of the times, and, in their own ludicrous or pathetic associations, furnishing the key wherewith to unlock the floodgates of public laughter or of public pity.

We are the creatures of Extremes: words feel this. They are the objects of our wildest caprice. Now honored and lionized—reveling in hut and hall, then cast aside and forgotten—damned so that prayers offered up in all churches would not save them. This Abuse of Words might add a strange chapter to the "Curiosities of Literature;" and I think it not at all improbable that one of the faithfulest indications of the tendency of popular feeling, and one of the truest sublimations of the hour or the Age are to be sought in our common, vulgar catch-words and bandied phrases—extravaganzas that seem to have no rationale, which appear amongst us as outlaws and rebels that acknowledge allegiance to no established power, but which come—shift and sway us—leave their momentary impression, and then go as they came—without announcement and without farewell.

In the time of Shakespeare, for instance, the employment of the word 'HUMOR' was carried to the most ridiculous excess. The 'fast' gents of those days had all their thousand and one 'humors' which they affected and pampered—any conceivable peculiarity or bizarrerie being, for the time their 'humor.' Nay, not only was it applied to idiosyncracies of character, but even *garters*, *hat-bands* and *shoe-ties* had each its particular 'humor'—so that it grew to be a perfect mania, "bred," as Ben Jonson tells us, "in the special galantry of our time, by affectation, and fed by folly."

This absurdity Shakespeare laughably exposes, in the character of Nym, whom he causes to discourse after the following fashion:—

"*Nym.* And this is true [To Page]. I like not the *humor* of lying. He hath wronged me in some *humors;* I should have borne the *humored* letter to her: but I have a sword and it shall bite upon my necessity. He loves your wife; there's the short and the long. My name is Corporal Nym; I speak and I avouch. 'Tis true:—my name is Nym, and Falstaff loves your wife.—Adieu! I love not the *humor* of bread and cheese; and there's the *humor* of it. Adieu.

Page. The humor of it, quoth 'a! here's a fellow frights *humor* out of its wits."

Merry Wives of Windsor, II. 1.

Wherein we most heartily agree with Page; but

we are *out of humor* with the wretched affectation, and can only exclaim, with honest Ben:

> "But that a rook, by wearing a py'd feather,
> The cable hat-band, or the three pil'd ruff,
> A yard of shoe-tye, or the Switzer's knot
> On his French garters, should affect a *humour*,
> O, it is more than most ridiculous!"
>
> *Induction to "Every Man out of his Humour."*

This is surely the very depth of bathos: and yet we have no lack of parallel terms to bear it company. Thus the verb 'ACCOMMODATE' was, about the same period, lugged into discourse on every proper or improper occasion—a word which, by the way, has, in our own day, become again popular and is now used almost as frequently, and quite as ineptly as of yore. Nor is it presumable that many of its modern abusers would be much more successful in defining it, in its multifarious applications, than was their grand prototype, Bardolph:

> "*Accommodated;* that is, when a man is, as they say, *accommodated;* or when a man is,—being,—whereby,—he may be thought to be—*accommodated;* which is an excellent thing."
>
> *Second Part of Henry IV.* III. 2.

The similarity of Ajax to *a jakes* furnished the wits of Elizabeth's reign with subject-matter for many a wretched pun, and gave the word a prodigious popularity, as we may see from the contemporary drama—ever the most faithful index of the tides of popular feeling. The occasion of all this pleasantry is generally ascribed to the "Metamorphosis of Ajax"—a tract published by Sir John Harrington, in which he gave an account of a novel invention . . . but we will not pursue the story!*

The Stage is the most merciless immolator of all fantastic and affected terms—just as, in its turn, the Green-room not unfrequently succeeds in imposing some of its own cant upon us. The History of Words, Idioms and Phrases that have thus been damned would be both varied and instructive. The usual mode is, of course, to take up the affectation and *run it to death*, and at the same time so to intertwine it with ludicrous associations that its use

* The tract was entitled "A New Discourse of a State Subject, called the Metamorphosis of Ajax:" and though the cause of many jokes to others, it was no joking to Sir John himself; for "Good Queen Bess," whose delicacy was offended, banished him from her sweet presence for some considerable time; nay, it is said he only escaped a star-chamber inquisition from the Queen's secret attachment to him. He was afterwards, however, recalled; on which occasion he affectingly describes his emotions as being those of "Saint Paul, when rapt up in the third Heaven!"

becomes forthwith more than hazardous. So was it with many of the absurdities ridiculed by Shakespeare and his cotemporaries—'*O Lord, sir,*' for instance, in *All's Well that End's Well.* Thus was it also with the once fashionable phrase, '*Egad and all that*'—which, it is said, the Duke of Buckingham's *Rehearsal* succeeded most effectually in putting an end to; while the once equally favorite, '*In fine, Sir,*' met a violent death at the hands of Dryden's *Sir Martin.* And every body knows how poor Thomson fared when his pathetic exclamation:

"O Sophonisba! Sophonisba O!"

was, by some wicked wight, travestied and repeated throughout all London in the shape of

"O Jemie Thomson! Jemie Thomson O!"

But these popular catch-words and phrases are universal in their rise and rule. They arise whenever, and at whatever, the public fancy is *tickled;* and are not without their own suggestive significance. "The most unobserved words in common use are not without fundamental meanings, however contemptible they may appear in this age of refinement," says Pegge.* Not at all to be slighted or despised, but worthy of most

* "Anecdotes of the English Language."

diligent investigation are these rich, ready-made idioms, begotten of the lusty needs of the times. For they prove assuredly more conclusively than could aught else, that no living Word is without its Logic and its Common Sense,—even though this Common Sense be, at times, of a very *un*common kind, and the train of Logic infinitely free and varied as the informign mind whence it springs.

Indeed many a time the most grotesque, the most fantastic words rest on a richer and more comprehensive insight and analogy than the more authoritative and classic part of speech. The popular phrase 'by hook or by crook' is an example to the point, having a curious genesis in the old forest customs, wherein persons entitled to fire-wood, in the king's forest, were only authorised to take of the dead wood, or branches of trees in the forest, "with a cart, a hook, and a crook." And how forcibly transferred thence to indicate gaining one's end as best he might. The phrase is of unknown antiquity. "Beastly Skelton" has this illustration:

> "Nor will suffer this boke
> *By hooke ne by crooke*
> Prynted for to be." *Colin Clout.*

The seemingly fantastic 'HONEY-MOON' is said to

owe its origin to a custom of an ancient Germanic people who were in the habit of drinking *mead* (in which *honey* was mingled) for thirty days after a wedding took place; and the ludicrous phrase to 'run-*amuck*' has its genesis in a positive ethnologic fact: the fact, namely, that among the Malays, a species of frenzy at times seizes individuals, and they run about committing indiscriminate murder (*amuck*). Johnson derives the expression to 'knock under' from "the submission expressed among good fellows by knocking under the table," and to '*go the whole hog*' is claimed, by an etymology I will not warrant, to owe its origin to a practice of the western butchers who ask their customer whether he will *go the whole hog* or deal only for joints or portions of it!

Often times, too, these every-day, bandied words and phrases have an expressive power that more elegant substitutes would but lamely realize. How significant, for instance, are 'close-fisted,' 'mealy-mouthed,' to 'rule the roast,' to 'egg on' (to anything), 'hood-wink,' 'quiz,' the 'hypoes,' 'bamboozle,' 'balderdash,' 'ink-horn' terms, 'fast' boys, 'rich' stories. So we speak of one's having 'brass' or 'tin,' or of one's being in a 'pickle;' and we exclaim 'ginger!' and we speak of a person in a state of intoxication (which, by the way, is related in its very origin to *poison*—toxicum) as being 'tight,' 'tipsey,' 'boosy, 'potvaliant,' 'muddled,' 'fuddled,' 'fou,' 'corned,' 'half seas over,' 'the worse for liquor,' 'drunk as a piper,' or as having a 'brick in his hat!' And how far might we go before we would find such expressive symbols as 'blue-stocking' (*bas bleu*) or 'hail-fellow,' or 'all the go,' or 'catch-penny,' or 'fire-eater,' or 'dead-letter,' (a term which the Post Office has given us?) or 'chatter-box,' or 'crusty,' or 'inuendo,' (literally a *nodding* at) or 'leg-bail,' or 'cut a swell,' or 'hobby,' or to 'palm,' (anything on one), or 'luggage,' which is just something *lugged* about! Though what special applicability there is in the old phrase 'honest as the skin between the brows,' it might be difficult to tell; and equally hard to tell how the phrase to 'sow one's wild oats' arose, and why it was that *oats* should have been selected from among grains as emblematic of the dissipation and excess of youth; while to 'curry favor,' smacks quite of the stable; the once popular exclamation, 'Cry you mercy, I took you for a joint stool,' seems purely fantastic, and I suppose brandy is called the *water of life*, 'eau de vie,' 'aqua vitæ,' 'usquebaugh,' (for they all have the same meaning) according to the law of *lucus a non*—precisely because it proves in so many cases the water of death!

There is another class of fantastics that also claims attention. I mean such as have been formed purely under the guidance of the ear—rhyming reduplicates, which have no meaning aside from what the mere sound carries with it. Such are 'bow-wow,' 'chit-chat,' 'harum-scarum,' 'flim-flam,' 'helter-skelter,' 'higgledy-piggledy,' 'hodge-hodge,' 'hubbub,' 'hurly-burly,' 'rif-raff,' 'tip-top,' 'rub-a-dub,' 'slip-slop,' (exemplified in Mrs. Malaprop in the *Rivals*) 'tip-top!'*

But I forget to mention the very term that most perfectly typifies many of the words of this Ramble. I mean 'GROTESQUE.' And indeed its origin is *grotesque* enough, being taken from certain whimsical figures found in the subterranean apartments—*grottoes*—in the ancient ruins at Rome, and thence extended to typify aught fantastic, ludicrous, or irregularly proportioned. Such is the derivation given by Benvenuto Cellini in his *Memoirs;* and as I have the passage at hand, I shall quote it: "These foliages have received the name of *grotesque* from the moderns because they are found in certain caverns in Rome, which in ancient days were chambers, baths, studies, halls and other places of the like nature. The curious

* Notes and Queries, vol. viii.

happened to discover them in these subterranean caverns whose low situation is owing to the raising of the surface of the ground in a series of ages, and as these caverns in Rome are commonly called *grottoes*, they from them acquire the name of grotesque." *

And numerous are the other words of equal interest, in which the workings of fairy Fancy may be traced. It was a piece of phantasy, for instance, to call the Roman platform for orators the 'ROSTRUM,' from the fact of its having been adorned with the *beaks* (*rostra*) or heads of captured ships, and I remember years ago feeling great pleasure at the perception of the connection—fanciful and yet faithful—of 'INCULCATE' with *calx*, the heel (*inculco*, to tread over again, to *heel*-it over again and hence to impress by frequent admonitions). What is a '*brown* study?' Is it a *barren* study, or is it allied to the word *brow?* Certainly 'etiquette' is just *the ticket:* it having been once the custom to get out cards containing orders for regulating ceremonies on public occasions. And 'COCKADE,' 'tis said, arose during the wars of the Scotch covenanters, when the English to distinguish

* Memoirs of Benvenuto Cellini, a Florentine Artist, written by himself, vol. I. p. 65.

them wore a black rosette, which from its position, shape, etc., the Scotch nicknamed *cock*'ade!*

But, beneath the lowest depth of vulgarity, slang and Billingsgate a lower deep opens in the expressive power of speech. For without the pale of civilization, in depths where not even

"The rarity
Of Christian charity"

penetrates, live brothers of ours, and children are born and live and die who speak not even the language of other men; but a speech of their own—dark and terrible and awfully significant. This Cant Language, or *Argot* we have, during the last few years, been made familiar with from the representations of popular novels. Eugene Sue, for example, has vividly portrayed the Parisian *langue des escrocs*—giving us an insight both into its dark and its bright side. For even it, 'twould seem, has its lights—its gleams of humanity—that manifest that its authors are still of our common kind, and that the germs of love and pity and hope are quite absent from no mortal breast.

* "Cocarde, touffe de rubans que sous Louis XIII. on portait sur le feutre, et qui imitait la crête du coq." Roquefort, *Dictionaire étymologique.*

Puns might form a characteristic and amusing topic for investigation under the Fantastic in Words, though it is entirely too ample a theme to admit of treatment here, approaching as I am towards the end of this Ramble. Did we enter into the subject in extenso we should assuredly begin with classic puns—Homer and the sons of the Tragic Muse having not disdained to quip and quibble—lingering over the graves of some of Cicero's most successful sallies (witness that wicked one on the Senator who was a tailor's son, *rem acu tetigisti*—you have touched the matter *sharply:* or, with the point of a *needle*)!* The archæology of Puns would moreover lead us to penetrate into the witticisms of the severe Milton—for even in *Paradise Lost* it would seem he punned and that horribly enough too. And then we should dive into the abyss profound of modern puns bringing up what pearls might offer themselves: and so should we have a complete history and philosophy of Puns and Punsters.

In the mean time I shall merely mention a few

* D'Israeli's "Curiosities." He cites Menage as saying: "I should have received great pleasure to have conversed with Cicero had I lived in his time. He must have been very agreeable in conversation, since even Cæsar carefully collected his *bons mots.*"

Etymologic or dead puns that occur to me, from Shakespeare.

Johnson asserts that a quibble was to Shakespeare he fatal Cleopatra for which he lost the world, and was content to lose it. This, like the generality of Johnsoniana, has considerable truth, with a vast deal of mere burly assertion and paradox about it. And I believe the question of Shakespeare's quibbles is now pretty much at rest.

In "As You Like It," Touchstone, the clown (and a very "material fool," by the way), says to Audrey: "I am here with thee and thy goats, as the most capricious poet, honest Ovid, was among the Goths."—*As You Like It*, III. 3.

Here the play of words between Goats and Goths is apparent enough: but the real pith and marrow of it is lost unless we recognize the occult pun that lurks in the term 'CAPRICIOUS'—the etymon of it—*Caper* (whence, I suppose, we have our verb to 'caper'—signifying a he-goat. This seen, the allusion becomes luminous.

Addison has announced that a pun cannot be translated. Literally, perhaps not. And yet skill and finesse can go wonderfully far towards a perfect rendering: for a proof of which we need go no farther than Schlegel's Translation of Shakespeare, wherein, though, of course, times innumerable he falls infinitely short, he attempts, at least, to render every *nuance* of expression and every finesse of verbal play. That they are many a time thin and ghostly must certainly be admitted, yet it must also be granted that his Translation is an example of what diligence *can*, in this direction, perform.

Puns are the most fickle and fragile things in existence. They live and move and have their being in *chance*. Hence it is not at all to be wondered at, should they many a time, in the lapse of years, perish through neglect. The word 'TANDEM' shuts up a curious practical pun, unrecognized till translated, and here is an example from the mouth of that monster of sin, sack and sagacity—Sir John Falstaff:

Chief Justice. You follow the young prince up and down like his *ill angel.*

Falstaff. Not so, my lord; your *ill angel* is light; but I hope he that looks upon me will take me without weighing; and yet, in some respects, I grant, I cannot go, I cannot tell.

Second Part of Henry IV. I. 2.

Here in order to appreciate the pun we must recollect that an 'Angel' was, at that time, the name applied to a coin, worth about ten shillings (English): the quibble, together with his not 'going' and not 'telling' (i.e. not passing current, not standing weight) then becomes luminous with meaning.

So do words fall into disuse, and are cast out as worthless and witless things. And this, too, in their old age, after a life-time's faithful service and too frequent abuse. They die with grief to see mere *parvenus* usurp their places—and find not even a champion to vindicate their cause or a historian to write their epitaph.

Yet sometimes they *do* find a defender. Pegge,* for instance, with much grave humor, pleads the cause of "Old, unfortunate and discarded words and expressions, which are turned out to the world at large, by persons of education (without the smallest protection), and acknowledged only by the humbler orders of mankind: who seem charitably to respect them as decayed gentlefolks that have known better days!"

* Anecdotes of the English Language.

RAMBLE EIGHTH.

VERBAL ETHICS.

"By your words ye shall be justified, and by your words shall ye be condemned."

SHALL we ascend to the highest statement and say that in Words there is an Ethical element also? For ever the innermost evolves itself and becomes the outermost; and surely it cannot be otherwise than that some transcript should be left in Words of the workings of that ethical Conscience that witnesses within us of right and wrong. Once, we know, every term, be it warped in its meaning, or be it meaningless, rushed forth, glowing and red hot, from the consciousness, laden with its own power and pathos—a blessing or a curse, a startling metaphor or a rich poetic image.

And so, too, we may read in Words the moralities of mankind. They are the decalogue in miniature—the verdicts pronounced by the great High Court of Humanity, not to be circumvented, and at once without precedent and without repeal. Oh! not unmindful be we of these still small voices, which, from cavernous depths, whisper to the willing ear, of human frailty and of human power—which, with a certain beautiful scorn, repel all meanness and ignobility, beckoning with alluring smiles to crowns and garlands starry and unfading, and telling of thee,

> "Stern Daughter of the voice of God,
> O Duty!"

It may be interesting, to begin with, to notice the evidence embalmed in Words of the primitive morality of mankind, and to trace the development of the historical conscience in its ascent to absolute ethical judgments. Marvelous are these vestiges of the spiritual history of man!

The law, which, in early times regulated the notions of guilt and innocence would not appear to have been very rigid. For if words speak truly 'INNOCENCE' itself merely consists in the not doing any harm—*in-nocens*—or, as we also say, 'harmless.' It is, therefore, a negative, not a positive virtue. 'GUILT' unfolds some curious historic and ethic facts. The Saxon form of the word is *gylt**—signifying both a

* From the verb *gyldan*, to pay. By the way, the ancient 'guild' is also formed from this verb; since each member of the fraternity was obliged to—*gyldan*—*pay* something.

crime and a *debt*, or *fine*—the latter, however, is the primary signification. It was, in fact, a *fine, or remuneration paid by a person who had committed some offense;* and then this *fine* applied to the *crime* itself. The person was brought in—gyltig—*guilty* of so much, that is, he was compelled to *pay* so much.* The attachment of a moral idea to a mere business transaction is curiously suggestive of many things. And by the way, our 'CRIME'—if *crimen* be connected with κρινω—may have a derivation quite analogous to the preceding. It is instructive also to note that the German for *debt* and *sin* is one and the same word—*schuld;* and thereby hangs a pun of Jean Paul Richter's. In the *Flegeljahre*, the reader will remember the following: "'The count,' said one, 'with *his* fortune, marries for beauty and accomplishments only, for he has ten times more money than the general has debts?' 'What then,' said an unmarried comedian, who always played the father, 'the beloved is charity itself and covers a multitude of—*schulden—debts* [or sins].'"†

A not uninteresting comparison might be instituted between the respective codes of *honor* of different

* See the interpretation of the expressions 'ware' and 'wite' in Fossil Histories.

† Walt and Vult, vol. I. 194.

peoples. I shall, however, merely indicate two: The Frenchman's 'honest' man—*un honnête homme*—implies a person who *tells the truth;* while the Englishman clusters all his ideas of *honesty* around the *abstaining from stealing!* 'VIRTUE' to the ancient Roman meant simply physical bravery—*manliness;* while to the æsthetic Italian *virtu* has acquired the signification of the love of the fine arts. And it is also worth noting that 'VALOR' simply means *worth*—an allusion carried out in *worship*, as we have before seen. A certain degree of *moderation* in behavior—enough, at least, to keep one within bounds—*modus*—the word-forming faculties have named 'MODEST.' Whatever is *becoming* (decet) they call 'DECENCY.' And what is above all seemly and graceful in walk and conversation is affirmed, both truthfully and beautifully, to be 'DECOROUS'—that which is as a—*decus*—ornament and embellishment to all the other graces. This primary meaning of the word we can understand from the old verb to *decore*, as thus:

"Which church he *decored* with many ornaments and edifices, especially the south side thereof."

Fuller's Worthies.

When a person desires to exact a degree of homage which we are *not wont* (*in-soleo*) to render, we very properly call this 'INSOLENCE'—though, by the way, 'INSOLENT' did not at first carry with it any other idea than that which is *unusual.* As for example, in the following passage quoted by Richardson:

> "The interpretor of Hans Bloome names it (Tænia) the top of a pillar, but very *insolently* [i. e. very *unusually*] it being indeed that small fascia part of the Doric architecture."
>
> *Evelyn on Architects and Architecture.*

Chaucer well expounds the word for us:

> "*Insolent* is he that despiseth in his judgment all other folk, as in regard of his value, of his conning, of his speking, and of his bering."
>
> *The Persones Tale.*

'INDOLENCE,' again, lets us into a rather curious ethical fact—the composition of *indolentia* being *in* and *dolentia*, that is to say *a freedom from pain!* Can it be that this circumstance induces and implies laziness or idleness? What a curious state of things is it, in which a *thoughtful* person becomes 'pensive;' when one who always *separates the truth*—se verus— is said to be 'severe;' when anything *shown* is regarded as a 'monster;' and when the entire notion of 'convivial' is that of *living together!* And yet is not 'comfort' very truly that wherewith we *strengthen* one another? So an 'agreeable' person is quite faithfully one who is suited—*a* (*notre*) *gré*—to our disposition—a man *after one's own heart*, as we say. And what a depth of meaning is there in the fact that 'study' is literally just zeal; while 'earnest' and 'yearning' are one word!

'NOBLE' declares itself to be primarily that which is *known*—noted—bruited about: so it would appear that language takes no cognizance of *hidden* worth, but conceives of all 'NOBILITY' merely as notoriety and measures all talent by success. And so—even as we should expect—'MEAN' declares itself to be that which appertains to the *mæneg*—οἱ πολλοί—the *many:* having its origin among the ignobile vulgus, *un*known and so not at all 'NOBLE.'

> "He was a veray parfit *gentil* knight."
>
> *Chaucer.*

'GENTIL' (*gentle*) is the Latin *gentilis* from *gens*, a clan—and so pertaining to a clan—'CLANNISH,' as the Scotch say. This is the primary signification. The transition in the meaning of this term—through which it has passed from one who has relation to *some* race (a 'HIDALGO,' as they say in Spain, that is a *son of something* in contradistinction to him who is a *son* *of nothing*), or *of birth*,* as we say, in opposition to him who is of no 'family,' down to its present vague, indefinite application or mis-application—might, had we opportunity to trace it, be not uninteresting or unprofitable. In the mean time take the following from *Froissart:*

> "Il-y-avoit un Chevalier, Capitaine de la Ville: point *gentil homme* n' estoit: et l'avoit fait, pour sa vaillance, le Roy Edouard Chevalier."
>
> *Chronicle* V. ii.

And there are other words that point the same moral. The striking analogy between *kin* and *kind* is significant, and 'GENEROUS' primarily means simply *of birth*. Shakespeare presents an example of its employment in this its primary sense. Thus Desdemona says:

> "How now, my dear Othello?
> Your dinner, and the *generous* islanders
> By you invited, do attend your presence."
>
> *Othello*, III. 2.

Here 'generous' necessarily implies '*noble*'—the

* If 'Gens' is from *gigno* (γίγνεο), these words do, in the last analysis, all merge into one; while the divers offshoots—'Gentle,' 'Genteel,' 'Gentile,' etc., all flow from one fountain.

islanders *of birth.* And more of the same: 'fame,' 'renown,' 'reputation.' 'REPUTATION' is simply what one is *reputed* (not at all affecting the 'character,' which is the *seal* and *token* impressed on the soul, organic in the structure of one's being: and so, independent of all 'reputation.') 'RENOWN' is, as we see, just the being *named over and over—renommé*, and 'FAME' itself (*fama, phemi*, to speak) is but the being *spoken about*, idle rumor, surely not to be very ardently coveted. Here is one of Carlyle's fiery fragments that lights up these words with luminous meanings: "So fares it with the sons of Adam in these bewildered epochs; so, from the first opening of his eyes in this world, to his last closing of them and departure hence, speak, speak, O speak; if thou have any faculty, speak it, or thou diest and it is no faculty! So in universities, and all manner of dames' and other schools, of the very highest class as of the very lowest; and Society at large, when we enter there, confirms with all its brilliant review-articles sncessful publications, intellectual tea-circles, literary gazettes, parliamentary eloquences, the grand lesson we had. Other lesson, in fact, we have none, in these times. If there be a human talent, let it get into the tongue, and make melody with that organ. The talent that can say nothing for itself, what is it?

Nothing; or a thing that can do mere drudgeries, and at best make money by railways."*

But we must ascend to the appreciation of the King-words of the moral world—of Good and Bad, of Truth and Right and Wrong—spinal expressions in the Ethical utterance of man. Of 'GOOD' the derivations are very varied. Richardson thinks it is from the Saxon verb *God*ian, to aid, to benefit. Skinner prefers to deduce it from the Latin *gaudeo.* Junius asserts it is from the Greek αγαθος—an opinion which Donaldson† also favors. Webster finds the primary meaning to be strong, free, large. And Horne Tooke assures us that it is "Ge-owed perhaps *gowed,* written and pronounced *Good,* which the Scotch pronounce and write *Gude.*" This is vague indeed: but no objection can be made to his derivation of 'BAD' which he thus evolves with his wonted sagacity: "To *Bay,* i.e. To vilify, to bark at, to reproach, to express horror, hatred and defiance, etc. *Bayed, Bœd,* i.e. *Bay'd, Ba'd,* abhorred, hated, defied, i.e. BAD."‡

'RIGHT' is no other than *rec*tum (*regitum*) the par-

* The "Stump Orator."

† New Cratylus, 420 and following.

‡ From the same verbal root come also 'Bane' and 'Ban: as thus—*Bayen, Bay'n, Bœn,* written BANE; To *ban,* to curse.

ticiple of the Latin verb *Regere* to order, to command! Whence the Italians have *ritto*, and from *Dirigere* comes *Dritto;* whence also the French have *droit* (old French *droict*). 'RIGHT' then is just what is *ordered, commanded, laid down* in the laws of eternal Justice, and 'LAW' and 'JUST' announce precisely the same high fact: 'JUST' is from jubere, *jussum*, and means the *commanded;* 'LAW' is from the Saxon verb *lecgan*, and implies something *laid down* as a rule of conduct. 'WRONG' is the past participle of the verb *wringan*, to *wring*, and means *wrung* or wrested from the *right* or ordered line of conduct.* *Wrung* was formerly written *wrong:* of this many certificates present themselves in our elder literature. Thus

"When your ignorant poetasters have got acquainted with a strange word, they never rest till they have *wrong* it in."
Ben Jonson, *Cynthia's Revels.*

Or thus from Chaucer,

"For which he wept and *wrong* his honde,
And in the bedde the bloody knyfe he fonde."
Man of Lawes Tale.

* Just as from *torquere* the Italians take *torto* and the French *tort*, wrong. *Diversions of Purley.*

Compare with 'RIGHT' and 'WRONG'—'upright,' 'regular,' 'rectitude,' 'error,' 'transgression' 'tortuous.' 'Upright' is palpable enough; 'regular' is according to *regula* or rule, and therefore according to the *ordered.* 'Rectitude' (*rectum*) is just the straight line—the *ordered* or *directed* one. 'Error' is an *erring* (erro)—a *wandering* from this straight line of 'rectitude.' 'Transgression' (*transgressum*) is a transgressing, a going beyond this *ordered* line. 'Tortuous' (*tort*, wrong) has also relation to what is *injurious* (*in jurem* against the law) that is against the *commanded*, that is *wrong.*

'MORAL' and 'ETHICAL' have a marvelous genesis. *Mores* in Latin means *customs; moralis*, the *customary:* and 'ETHICAL' is precisely the same word with a Greek origin—*ethikos, ethos!* On which words read this fiery comment: "Instead of shrieking more, it were perhaps edifying to remark, on the other side, what a singular thing *customs* (in Latin *mores*) are; and how fitly the virtue, manhood, or worth, that is in a man, is called his *morality* or *customariness.* Fell slaughter, one of the most authentic products of the pit, you would say, once give it customs, becomes war, with laws of war, and is customary and moral enough; and red individuals carry the tools of it girt round their haunches not without an air of pride—

which do thou nowise blame. While, see! so long as it is but dressed in hodden or russet; and revolution, less frequent than war, has not yet got its laws of revolution, but the hodden or russet individuals are uncustomary—Oh, shrieking, beloved brother blockheads of mankind, let us close those wide mouths of ours; let us cease shrieking, and begin considering!"

Great, good, glorious Carlyle! forced thyself, by thy longing and tameless heart, to set thyself in stern hostility to very many of the 'customs' and not a few of the 'moralities' of this our era—honest to the very profundity of thy great heart, yet thereby forced sometimes to appear dishonest—the wisest, and yet willing to be to many a stumbling-block and the foolishest—the most religious, and yet compelled to seem the most sacrilegious! with what Titanic force dost thou wield thy 'winged words,'—that in thy hands split oft with bursting, burning meaning: bringing them up in their primitive truth-loving and truth-telling simplicity, and setting them, not without a certain grave sarcastic smile, over against their abuses and their corruptions and their twistings to gild a falsehood or to consecrate a lie—there to blazon in immortal scorn human hypocrisies and shams!

And 'TRUTH,' too, how pregnant its meaning! 'TRUTH' is that which a man *troweth*, thinketh, firmly believeth:* 'TRUE,' or *trew* as it was formerly written,

("A bedrole long and *trew* he reckoneth")

is that which is *trewed* or firmly believed! Thus 'TRUTH' and the 'TRUE' suppose humanity: they express man, his limitations, struggles, aspirations. For how possible is it for one to *trow* what is not in the highest translation *true!* And indeed the word primarily carries with it no absolute force—a *false truth*, that is a false opinion, a false belief, being an expression not unfrequently met with in our elder literature. Thus

"Many a *fals treuthe.*"

Piers Ploughman.

But here it is that the marvel and miracle of language begin. For the divine influx, working on the unfolding Conscience and the ascending Spirituality of man, is constantly operating to elevate and ennoble words. How often do Words, through the inspiration that is breathed into them, become virtuous and valorous beyond their native ability. They lend

* The past participle of the verb to *trow* was formerly written *trew*, just as the past participle of *know* is written *knew*.

themselves plastic to the moulding power of something higher than human Will. For man cannot free himself from God. The spell of divinity is on him.

> "The hand that rounded Peter's dome,
> And groined the aisles of Christian Rome,
> Wrought in a sad sincerity:
> Himself from God he could not free;
> He builded better than he knew,
> The conscious stone to beauty grow!"

And so, through these Symbols glimmer hints of deeper meanings—sacred suspicions of divinity—trailing clouds of glory: so that

> "We stand,
> Adore and worship, when we know it not;
> Pious beyond the intention of our thought,
> Devout beyond the meaning of our will."

For if we saw that 'Moral' and 'Ethical' meant merely the customary and the capricious, yet do they bear the burden of something stabler by far—of laws in the depths of the divine consciousness which no caprice creates nor custom changes. 'Truth' but implies that which each man *troweth* or believeth for himself—and so would seem to be a fickle and fanciful enough affair: 'virtue' may have been to the old warlike Roman nothing nobler than his *vir*tus or *man*liness; to the art-enamored Italian his *virtu*, or dilettanteism, and to the eupeptic Yankee his plenty of pork and beans: yet is there a 'TRUTH' that has not its warranty in the partial views of this man or that, but which firmly plants itself on the Central and the Unconditioned; there is a 'VIRTUE' which is neither Greek nor barbarian nor bond nor free—

> "For its source from without rises never;"

but which is inherent in the very build of the world.

There is oft times even something godlike in the contempt with which words themselves look down upon all meanness and littleness. For, if they be, alas, all too frequently, the slaves of falsehood, they are none the less many a time the first and final refuge of truth. With what scorn, for example, are 'VANITY' and 'VAUNTING' viewed when we perceive that they are both the offspring of *vanus*, empty, and regard them in their true character as mere emptiness! How perfect, too, is the sentence we pronounce whensoever we speak of a 'MISER,' even if we do not always recognize that we just characterize him as a wretched, a *miser*able one. In this very sense Shakespeare and Spenser and Sidney many a time employ it:

"Decripit *miser!* base, ignoble wretch!"
First Part of Henry VI. V. 5.

"Do not yet disdaine to carrie with thee the wofull words of a *miser* now disparing."
Arcadia, p. 117.

In both of these instances the word has no connection with avarice—implying simply a *wretched* one. And the love of money cannot conceal from us that it is at least a very 'SORDID' thing; and *sordid* is of a base enough extraction—claiming kinship with *sordes*, which is just *filth!*

Indeed there often lurks in words a sly piece of sarcasm on pettiness or paltriness which shows that, how much soever Society may be sunk in inanity, they will yet continue to speak out boldly and truthfully. Might one not, to be charitable, admit that those mournful mementoes yclept 'DANDIES,' are in their very name, sufficiently afflicted—when we reflect that though it be *French*, it is only French for a *ninny—dandin:* Webster himself defining it as "a fop; a coxcomb; one who dresses himself like a doll *and who carries his character on his back!*" Again, how significant a moral is enwrapt in the fact that 'loose,' 'lose' and 'loss' are all from one root; that 'sore' and 'sorrow' have a like genesis. Who could wish any severer punishment on a 'PROFLIGATE' than that he is one whom the appellation itself declares to be dashed to the ground—*profligatus*—utterly broken and abandoned! And how fearfully are the *gnawings* of Conscience which attend the commission of any unmanliness or ungodliness embodied in our 'REMORSE!'

Thus do Words become most powerful engines in the cause of truth—flails with which shams and meannesses are castigated. On this head De Quincey discourses wisely:

"The word *humbug*, for instance, rests upon a rich and comprehensive basis: it cannot be rendered adequately, either by German or by Greek, the two richest of human languages, and without this expressive word we should all be disarmed for one great case, continually recurrent, of social enormity. A vast mass of villany, that cannot otherwise be reached by legal penalties or brought within the rhetoric of scorn, would go at large with absolute impunity were it not through the stern *Rhadamanthean* aid of this virtuous and inexorable word."*

'HUMILITY' is an instructive word, claiming kinship with *humus*, the ground—a lowly enough origin truly. 'PROBITY,' too, is just what has been *probed*,

* From a paper on "Language."

tried and found good; 'IMPERTINENT' is what does not *pertain*, does not belong to the occasion. 'MISERY,' it would seem, clusters all its associations around the *being hated* (miser, miseo?)—that being regarded as the worst of all *miseries*. And how full of significance is the term 'HAPPY!' If the testimony of language is to be received, it is a very indefinite affair indeed, being merely the abounding in *haps* or chances —not *mis*-haps, it is presumable: and yet the whole is just a great per*haps!* For thus expounds Paley:

> "The word *happy* is a relative term; in strictness any condition may be denominated *happy* in which the amount or aggregate of pleasure exceeds that of pain; and the degree of happiness depends upon the quantity of the excess."
>
> *Moral Philosophy*, book I.

O, not a dead letter, these living statutes of Words, but glowing and palpitating, laden with pathos and power, rich with the tragedy of souls!

Profoundly significant, too, is it to muster words with reference to the traces of the workings of the hot passion, the prejudice, the depravity, shall we say? of human nature.

Why, for instance, should a *judgment beforehand* be with us always a 'PREJUDICE,' unless it be that we are more apt to judge ill than well? Why cannot a man be *spirited* and courageous without converting the disposition into 'ANIMOSITY? What causes a 'cupidity' in the way of benevolence or a 'lust' of doing good to sound like incongruities or downright contradictions? What a story of covetousness and extortion is revealed by such a word as 'USURY' —which should surely be called *abusury* at once! Or, again, why is it that we cannot promulgate anything with reference to a person, without forthwith falling to 'TRADUCE' him? or report a story without becoming 'TELL-TALES'—while 'STORY' itself is now quite synonymous with a *fib*.

Under old Roman rule persons who were set free from servitude—*freed-men*—were called *libertini*; but does that authorize us to convert them into 'LIBERTINES'—or, is there a dark current of wickedness underflowing all this—*must* liberty degenerate into license? *Mignon* in French and *mignone* in Italian both imply a *darling*, a *favorite*; but since

> "That poor man
> That hangs on princes' favors"

is not apt to be over scrupulous touching the mode in which he gains these favors, it gradually came by a regular process of degradation to bear with it all the baseness and blackness of a 'MINION!' If pretense and presumption be not all too rife, as well now as among the old Hellenic sages, why is it that the appellation of a *wise man* should be loaded with contempt—that he should become a mere mock wise man (which is the foolishest of all)—a mere 'SOPHIST,' and all his instructions mere 'SOPHISTRIES?' And in our own times we may discern the same principle at work —so that the very *exercise of reason* we are fain to stigmatize as 'RATIONALISM.' It would seem impossible for one to hold an *opinion* without converting it into a 'DOGMA,' or assert one without becoming 'DOGMATICAL;' to be habile or business-like without its merging into the 'PRAGMATICAL;' and I know not as it is possible to *advance* without being 'FORWARD!'

The original signification of 'OFFICIOUS' we know to have been merely dutiful, attentive—full of *offices.* Thus I find in Dr. Johnson's poem on his servant, Levett:

> "Well tried through many a varying year,
> See Levett to the grave descend;
> *Officious*, innocent, sincere,
> Of every friendless name the friend!"

But how different its present application! Why is it that we convert a *feeling over again* into a 'RESENTMENT;' that we cannot *turn the mind to* (animadverto) a person or thing, without 'ANIMADVERTING' thereon, or have a conception without getting into 'CONCEIT' with it? while even the *sacred* and the *holy* will degenerate into the merely 'SANCTIMONIOUS!'

What a tale of strength abused does '*robust*ious' tell us; and what a history of pettifogging do 'CUNNING' and 'CRAFTY' tell!—'CRAFTY' which is properly just skillful, powerful, 'artful' (only that *that* also has gone the same way); and 'CUNNING' which, at first was simply—*connan*—*kenning*—*knowing:* but, indeed, I despair of defining the word, since almost every analogue that can be enumerated has been equally debased: for what does a 'knowing' fellow mean but an artful, 'designing'* fellow? A similar and even sadder debasement is observable in the word 'SENSUAL,' which as we have before seen, strictly signifies simply that which pertains to the *senses*—sensualis—but which has so completely taken possession of and fortified itself within the corrupt acceptation that we are fain to invent 'SENSUOUS' to supply its place. Surely, surely, Dan Chaucer spake rightly—

"To don sinne is mannish!"†

* Certain it is that his 'designs' will be *bad.*

† Take in addition, such examples as 'MENIAL,' 'NIGGARD,' 'PIETIST,' 'TAX,' 'TRAITOR,' 'TREASON,' 'SEMBLANT,' 'PERJURE,' etc.

We find at once our compensation and our consolation in scrutinizing to the bottom the abyss, black and bottomless though it may seem. For soon light begins to blend with the shade, aurora-streaks of hope become visible and the white butterflies of Love flutter gaily in the ruddy sunlight. For if it be in reality that there is nothing totally bad—if our Life-tree bear on its boughs at once the blossoms of Good and Evil; so, while we find in language, traces of baseness and corruption—if words appear subservient to everything that is mean and contemptible, they also lend themselves graciously, and, as it were, with a greater good will, to keep or carry sentiments of Love, of Peace, of Hope, of Benevolence, of Nobility; and the same breath that festers into a curse can beautifully mould itself into a heaven-born aspiration and become the swift-footed and winged messenger of truth and benignity!

What is 'DUTY?' Is it not evidently what a man owes (*devoir*, *du*)—all that is *due* from him to himself and to others. High, clear above us sounds the voice of the dread eternal Nemesis—unflinching, exacting, with trumpet-tones demanding "What thou owest!"

> "Stern Lawgiver! yet thou dost wear
> The Godhead's most benignant grace;

Nor know we anything so fair
 As is the smile upon thy face:
Flowers laugh before thee on their beds,
And fragrance in thy footing treads;
Thou dost preserve the stars from wrong;
And the most ancient heavens, through Thee, are fresh and strong."*

How severe and stately is 'MANLY,' which is just *man-like:* how noble, how compensating! It strengthens our faith in human nature! And so, like to a fair lily, springing up amid carnage and corruption comes such a word as 'CREDIT'—which is just the—*credit*-um—the *belief*, or 'trust' we have in the honor and good faith of our fellows. So that even all the truckling and prevarication of commerce and politics cannot conceal from us that there is still among men a great 'credit' or *trust* system; that we have not yet lost all faith in each other, in spite of all failures!

If there are those that are 'MALEVOLENT' or *ill*-willed, have we not, also, the 'BENEVOLENT,' or those that wish us *well;* and, if there be *man-haters*—'MISANTHROPISTS,' be there not also, *man-lovers*—'PHILANTHROPISTS?'—the good making up for the evil; the bad pole of existence balanced by the opposite good pole. In fine what could be more beautiful than

* Wordsworth: Ode to Duty.

those two words—'COMPASSION' and 'SYMPATHY'—both of which imply a fellow-suffering—a *fellow-feeling*—and which sound forth here with the soft, wailing melody of an infinite, world-embracing pity? Thus teach they us that, while from our lone Valley of the Shadow of Death ascendeth ever to heaven the tear-steeped tones of mankind's *miserere*—like to the "infinite inarticulate grief and weeping of forsaken children:" yet are we not utterly orphaned and alone; but still in unison with our sorrows tremble ever the sympathizing tones of

"The slow, sad music of humanity."

And are we not sure that every one of our pangs is known and felt by Him whose Heart is a Heart of Compassion?

RAMBLE NINTH.

MEDALS IN NAMES.

'Omnibus est nomen, sed non idem omnibus omen.

"WHAT'S in a name?" asks Juliet, powerfully affected by the thought that that which we appellate a rose, by any other cognomen would possess the property of titillating the olfactory in an equally dulcet manner.

In all seriousness, much and much is in a name. That Quaker individual understood its power when he threatened the canine quadruped with condign visitation, and suggested, "I will not kill thee, but I will give thee a bad *name!*"

The lordship of Names is the most absolute and universal in the realm of human tyrannies. Never was autocrat half so despotic as those airy kings that lord it over man's thought. Of how many million toiling brains is it the ambition merely to make a *name;* and Roderigo felt that, robbed of his 'good name,' he was 'poor indeed!'

What comes so close to man or woman as his or her Name? Next to the sweet consciousness of identity, of this "pleasing, anxious being" is the marvel and mystery of one's Name. The tragedy of tragedies is in a Name. To what thrilling realizations may it lift—raising

"Beyond the reaches of the soul."

Names of home—the sacred names of mother and sister and wife—the sweet idyl of the names of children—the clustering associations of the names of the troop of amis! Names of bards, benefactors, martyrs, dear to the heart of the world—Names of the primeval supremes, of the founders of the antique Religions: Brama, Osiris, Zoroaster, Prometheus, Orpheus, Jove! The execrated names of tyrants and oppressors—names uttered with compressed lips—names of warriors and conquerors writing their fiery legends on man's mind as the lightning writes on rocks! Names of the dead—names embalmed—tombs in a battle-field, o'ergrown with grasses and flowers!

Of the suggestions from names none are more significant than such as arise from a mustering of names that have been lifted out of their appellative import and incorporated as common nouns—*nomina realia*—in our language. This interesting class of words is quite numerous: I shall mention such as occur to me just now.

And here one's associations of the antique come in and suggest such examples as 'TANTALIZE,' from Tantalus, whose dreadful punishment it was to be continually in sight of water etc. and yet never allowed a drop thereof; Hermes, primeval chemist, has given us 'HERMETIC;' Hercules has given us 'HERCULEAN' and Academus 'ACADEMY;' then, Gordius, the Phrygian king, has left us the legacy of that famous 'GORDIAN' knot; Mausolus is immortal in his 'MAUSOLEUM;' Epicurus survives in 'EPICURE,' and Demosthenes thunders still and 'fulmines over Greece' in 'PHILIPPIC.' And more: 'PROMETHEAN,' 'PLATONIC,' 'BACCHANALIAN' are palpable; Atlas, on whose shoulders rested the pillars of heaven, has given us 'ATLAS;' a 'VOLCANO' claims kinship with Vulcan; 'OCEAN' is quite as plainly very closely allied to Oceanus, and does not the god Terminus stand watcher over every one of our railroad stations? But to come to more modern contributions. 'GALVANISM' and 'MESMERISM' are palpable enough—being merely the *ism* devised by Galvani and Mesmer. Macadam has given us to 'MACADAMIZE;' Mackintosh has left his name to a coat, and Lord Spencer to the 'SPENCER.' Was the 'NEGUS' first compounded, as is asserted, by a Colonel Negus? We certainly know that Lord Sandwich has left his name to slices of bread and meat—'SANDWICH.' The associations we call 'TONTINE' were first conceived by a Neapolitan named Tonti; Dahl, a Swede, introduced the cultivation of the 'DAHLIA,' and Lord Orrery was the first for whom an 'ORRERY' was made.

The same law in the formation of words is frequently found in the genesis of terms that have acquired a degree of opprobrious or abusive signification. And often do words thus formed do sad injustice to their sires. Thus *Duns* Scotus, that subtilest of schoolmen, survives only in the shape of a 'DUNCE;' while Hector, son of Priam—a man who, it is said, united

"The mildest manners with the bravest mind"—

has received a maligned immortality in our verb 'To *Hector*' and a *hectoring* fellow, which is just a "blustering, turbulent, noisy fellow!" *Rodomont*—that celebrated hero in Ariosto—has lent us several words.

The name itself "rodomont" we take to designate a vaporing bully and boaster; and the very sublimation of empty bluster and rant we express by 'rodomontade.'

'FUDGE' is a curious word, having a positive personality underlying it. Such at least is it, if D'Israeli's account thereof be authentic. He quotes from a pamphlet published at the beginning of the Eighteenth Century, entitled "Remarks upon the Navy," the author of which says: "There was, sir, in our time, one *Captain Fudge*, commander of a merchantman, who upon his return from a voyage, how ill fraught soever his ship was, always brought home his owners a good cargo of lies; so much that now, aboard ship, the sailors, when they hear a great lie told, cry out, 'You fudge it!'"

The term 'CHOUSE,' a word which one used to hear on the lips of youngsters, has a similar fantastic genesis in the Turkish name for interpreter—*chiaous*. It was a person holding this office in the Turkish embassy in England, and who in the early part of the Seventeenth century committed an enormous fraud on the Oriental merchants resident in London, that gave rise to this appellation as the designation for any huge piece of swindling. And Verstegan traces 'RIBALD' to an analogous origin—a derivation we are forced to hold by somewhat freely, but which none the less excellently illustrates the principle now under exemplification. But let him speak for himself.

"This word was at first *Rabad* as yet in the Netherlands it is used, wherehence both wee and the French having taken the name, have somewhat varied it both in ortography and sence. It was the proper name of *Rabad*—a heathen king of Friesland, which being instructed in the faith of Christ, by the godly Bishop Ulfrau faithfully promised to be baptized, and appointed the time and place: where being come, and standing in the water, hee asked of the Bishop where all his forefathers were that in former ages were deceased? the Bishop answered, that dying without the true knowledge of God etc. they were in hell, then quoth Rabad, I hold it better and more praiseworthy to go with the greater multitude to hell, then with your few Christians to heaven; and therewithall he went out of the water unchristened [that is not brought over to the faith of *Christ:* to 'christen' being just to *Christ*-en]; and returned both to his wonted idolatry and to his evil lyf, notwithstanding the good admonitions of the Bishop, and an evident miracle, which (through the power of God) the said Bishop wrought, even in his own presence. Hee was afterwards surprised [literally *sur-prised* i. e. *over-taken*] with a suddaine and improvyded [i. e. *unforeseen*] death, about the year of our Lord 720, and his very name became so odious through his wickedness, that it grew to bee a tytle of reproche and shame, and hath so continued ever since."*

And the contributions from proper names are not exhausted. Into what an unenviable notoriety has the Trojan Pandarus been taken up in our term to 'PANDER;' and what centuries of political finesse are summed up in 'MACHIAVELISM'—offspring of that subtle Italian brain! One would not desire to share the fate of Dr. Guillotin and father such a word as 'GUILLOTINE.' So, *Solomon* is a common nickname for a blockhead; Cervantes has made 'QUIXOTIC' an epithet of universal significance, and our rich, rough New York life has erected 'MOSE' into a type of character which no other term could convey with equal directness and force. 'JESUIT' is another word of kindred genus. Its history too is important. It was, we know, the name given to the order instituted by Ignatius Loyola, in 1534. This order was called the *Society of Jesus*—and the members thereof 'Jesuits.' So much for the origin of the word. And now when we look in our dictionaries and find 'Jesuit' synony-

* Restitution of Decayed Intelligence, 337.

mous with *crafty intriguer*, and see 'Jesuitical' defined as 'designing; cunning; deceitful; prevaricating,' who could be persuaded that *these* are the characteristics and *these* the followers of that meek and lowly *Jesus*, in whose mouth no guile was found?

The American contributions to this class of words have been by no means scanty. Indeed, is it not natural that a people so prolific as are we in *isms* should leave a pretty large verbal precipitate? '*Bowey*-knife' is a familiar example of this kind. 'LYNCHING' smacks of the rude, lawless Western and Southern life, where immortal *Lynch* presides; while *Barnum* will live in his name and his *ism*, long after the 'happy family' shall have had its quietus, and the portals of the memorable 'Temple of the Moral Drama' shall have been closed for ever!

Sometimes, too, this process of word-building leads into fantastic snatches of life and thought. The word 'PASQUIN' is an example to the point having an exceedingly curious origin. The word was applied to a mutilated statue at Rome, in a corner of the palace Ursini, so called from a cobbler of the name of *Pasquin* who was remarkable for his sneers and gibes, and near whose shop the statue was dug up. On this statue it has been customary to paste satiric papers.

Hence, a lampoon.* In reading the elder Dramatists one very often lights upon the expressions '*Cain*-colored' and '*Judas*-colored'—forms which might be apt to puzzle us, did we not remember that all legends ascribe *red hair and beards* to both Cain and Judas; and, indeed, the aversion which our ancestors had for red or yellow hair was only less violent than the *odium theologicum*—so violent was it that they even favored the de'il himself with the attribute. To what is this owing? Had its association with the Danes, whom Alfred calls the *Heathen* Folk, anything to do with the prejudice?

What a profound significance frequently attaches to national names! What a host of ideas, for example, cluster around the 'SAXONS'—especially if we derive the name from *seax*, a sword: and so, *the men of the sword!* Readily can we understand how, with sword in hand, they became invincible in arms—driving all before them; and appreciate how those terrible Vikings, with their awful 'berserkir rage' spread dread and destruction all around the coasts which they haunted; and by the terror of their name, compelled the Gauls to intercalate, into their litany, a new petition: "A furore Normannorum, libera nos,

* Encyclopædia Americana.

Domine!" *Deliver us, O Lord, from tne fury of the Northmen!* For how could it be otherwise than that men who affected such grim appellations as 'BLOODY-AXE,' 'SKULL-CLEAVER,' 'DEATH'S HEAD' —and whose deeds did not belie their names, should inspire a natural horror? So with the 'PICTS,' the original (Welsh) forms of which Verstegan affirms to be Phictian i.e. *fighters;* and the 'SCOTS' which, according to the same authority, comes from the Teutonic verb scytan—*to shoot.*

On the word 'SLAVE' Gibbon, in the Fifty-fifth Chapter of the "Decline and Fall," has a pungent passage which I shall quote here as altogether pertinent. "The unquestionable evidence of Language attests the descent of the Bulgarians from the original stock of the Sclavonic, or more properly Slavonic race: and the kindred tribes of Servians, Bisneans, Rasivians, Croatians, Walachians etc., followed either the standard or the example of the leading tribe. From the Euxine to the Adriatic, in the state of Captives, or Subjects, or Allies, or Enemies, in the Greek Empire, they overspread the land; and the national appellation of the SLAVES has been degraded by chance or malice from the signification of glory to that of servitude."*

* "Decline and Fall of the Roman Empire," Vol. VII. Chap.

A mere chance, then, a mere mishap in war has given us the appellation of 'SLAVE;' and those old *Slavic* tribes, subdued, stolen and sold, have immortalized their name, and within it embalmed the record of mankind's infamy.

We are not without analogues to this same mode of procedure. Thus the 'HELOTS,' among the Greeks, were, it is asserted, simply the Εἵλωτες—that is, the

55. In a note to the above he says: "Jordan subscribes to the well-known and probable derivation from *slava, laws, gloria*, and which forms the termination of the most illustrious names (De Originibus Sclavonicis Pars I. p. 40; pars IV. p. 101, 102)."

An example of the employment of this word *slava*, glory, occurs in Suwarrow's letter to the Empress Katharine on the taking of Ismael, wherein he exclaims:

"*Slava* Bogu! *slava* vam!
Krepost vzata, y ia tam."
Glory to God; *glory* to thee!
The fortress is taken and I am there.

The correctness of this derivation has, however, latterly been called in question by some philologers. Anent which take the following from Talvi's "Literature of the Slavic Nations." "The name of the *slavi* has generally been derived from *slava*, glory, and their national feelings have of course been gratified by this derivation. But the more immediate origin of the appellation is to be sought in the word *Slovo*, word, speech," etc.

Lit. of Slav. Nat. p. 2, 3, *note.*

dwellers in *Helos*—a town in Laconia—to whom, perchance, a similar mishap arrived: and so 'HELOT' came to be used in precisely the sense in which we employ 'SLAVE.'

It by no means unfrequently occurs that national names thus become the type of particular qualities, or characteristics, or dispositions. Thus the *Franks* give us our adjective 'FRANK,' with the French 'franc' whence is, perhaps, also, our English 'FREE.' If so, then both 'SLAVE' and 'FREE' have their origin in national appellations. The *Greeks* have always been regarded as a jolly, luxurious race: so much so, that the Latins employed the verb *Græcari* (lit. *to play the Greek*) to designate fine living and free potations, a sense in which Horace frequently uses it; while Shakespeare often mentions the 'merry Greeks,' and, even in England, 'as merry as a Greek' was long a favorite allusion. The poor *Trojans*, however, have not fared quite so well—sinking down even to the level of a *thief*. As when bully Pistol says,

> "———Dost thou thirst, base *Trojan*,
> To have me fold up Parca's fatal web?"
>
> *Henry V.* V. 1.

So, too, we have 'TURKS' whose savage disposition is of native growth; 'GASCONADE' from the lips of those on whom the sun of *Gascony* never shone; and 'TARTARS' who never saw *Tartary*. By the way what a keen set of fellows those Tartars must be, when 'to catch a *Tartar*' becomes so pungent an expression! Were the Carthaginians really instinctively liars, or was it only Roman malignity that made the '*Punic faith*' emblematic of utter national mendacity? Still do the 'GOTHS' and 'VANDALS' survive as typical of everything that is ferocious and sacrilegious, albeit between us and them rolls the flood of fourteen centuries; and it is even said that the 'OGRES' of the *Arabian Nights* are not merely mythic monsters, but that a dim memory survives of an Asiatic nation called the *Oïgours* who, along with the Huns and the Eastern barbarians, spread terror throughout Europe—leaving behind them mementoes and associations which became the bases of a thousand fairy and fantastic tales.

'PATAVINITY' (*Patois*) with which Livy was charged is plainly just that peculiar dialect spoken in *Patavium*, where Livy was born. So, 'LACONIC' —λαχωνιχος—is just something short and pithy—such as we might expect from the people of *Laconia*—the Spartans—a grave, sententious, silence-loving, and most Carlylean race. Again, the term 'CRAVAT' Skinner derives from the *Croat* soldiers, or *cravates*, as the French called them, though with how much probability the reader will judge for himself.*

In regard to the origin of the name 'GAULS' genia old Rabelais—who to the universality of his knowledge added an acquaintance with Philology—has a fanciful, though interesting enough passage, in which he traces the name to *Gala*, white: "Cest la cause pourquoy *Galli* (ce sont les Francoys, ainsi appellez parce que blancz sont naturellement comme laict, que les Grecz nomment *Gala*) voulentiers portent plumes blanches sur leurs bonnetz. Car, par nature, ilz sont ioyeulx, candides, gratieux et bien esmez; et pour leur symbole et insigne, ont la fleur plus que nulle aultre blanche, cest le lys."

This derivation is about as good as that of some high-minded Scots who attempt to prove that 'SCOTLAND' comes from Scota the (sham) daughter of Pharaoh, King of Egypt, married to Gaithelus, son of Cecrops, founder of Athens! or that of the Welsh-

* See Skinner's Etymologicon, *in loco.* Menage takes the word from the same source—saying thereanent: "On l'appelle de la sorte, à cause que nous avons emprunté cette sorte d'ornement des *Croates*, qu'on appelle ordinairement *cravates.*" Thus called because we borrowed that species of ornament which we commonly call '*cravats*' from the *Croats.*

Origines de la Langue Française.

man who deduced 'APOLLO' from *Ap-haul*—son of the sun! And yet these are no more ambitious than the magnificent names assumed by many of our Indian tribes, or by the Asiatics: instance the 'RAJPOOTS'—which, indeed, is nothing less lofty than the *Sons of Kings!*

Such are some of the most significant importations into our language from personal names. Names of places have been almost equally prolific. And most prominent among these are the names of inventions that have taken rise from the locality embodied in their appellations. Such terms as 'DAMASK' (*Damascus*); 'CURRANTS' (*Corinth*); 'HOLLAND;' 'NANKEEN' (*Nankin*); 'CALICO' (*Calicut*); to 'JAPAN;' 'BAYONET' (*Bayonne*); 'TURKEY;' with the names of liquors, such as 'PORT' (*Oporto*); 'COGNAC;' 'BURGUNDY' etc., etc., make themselves apparent at first sight.

Again, a 'CORDWAINER,' the technical term for a *shoe-maker*, plainly declares himself to be a worker in *cordwain*, or leather of *Cordova*, in Spain. Whence also the French 'CORDONNIER.' The 'ARRAS,' or hanging of tapestry—a word frequently employed by the elder dramatists—is evidently named after the city of *Arras*, in the French Netherlands. A 'CREMONA' violin unerringly points to its source. So does an 'ANDREW FARRARA.' And so also does a '*Douay*-BIBLE'—evidently being the translation made at *Douay*. Lunier declares 'MUSLIN' (what the French call *mousseline*) to be from *Moussoul*, in Mesopotamia; and asserts that 'PARCHMENT' is named after *Pergamus*—whose king, Eumenes, 'tis said, invented the article. But however this may be, a 'MAGNET,' at least points straight to *Magnesia*, in Asia Minor. Every 'GUINEA' we handle jogs the memory in regard to its origin on the *Guinea* coast—that ancient El Dorado, while our 'DOLLAR' (Swedish *daler*) is maintained by some to be connected with *Dale*, where, they say, it was first coined. And 'STERLING' may have some relation to the place of that name—though more probably, as Camden declares, it is a contraction from *Easterling*, "once the popular name of German traders in England, *whose money was of the purest gold.*"

It not unfrequently happens, too, that these appellations having their origin in the names of places, preserve some important piece of history. The word 'TARIFF' is an example to the point. It traces itself back to *Tarifa*, a Moorish name for a fortress on a Southern promontory of Spain, running into the Straits of Gibraltar, and commanding the entrance of the Mediterranean sea. From this *Tarifa* the Moors, during their dominion in Spain, were wont to watch merchant-ships passing into or out from the Mediterranean, and, making a sally therefrom, used to levy duty on merchandise carried by the ships. And from this practice it was that the application of the word 'TARIFF' arose.

Proper names! This is a vast, indeed a quite boundless field! A calculation that seems to err on the safe side makes out the number of surnames in the English language to be between *thirty and forty thousand!** Of English Surnames we have, so far, nothing like an adequate History or Philosophy. Camden†—"nourice of antiquitie"—broke ground more than two hundred years ago in this interesting investigation. His contemporary, genial old Verstegan, did good service in the same direction. On these—added to additional contributions of minor note—Mr. Mark Antony Lower wrought in the production of his "Essays on Family Nomenclature' (2 vols. 12mo., London, 1842). The Essays are useful and entertaining, though quite inadequate, Mr. Lower

* Rev. Mark Noble: *History of the College of Arms.*

† REMAINS *concerning Britaine*, but especially England and the Inhabitants thereof.

being no philologer. A work up to the demands of the theme would be indeed a desideratum.

Was there ever a time when men were anonymous?—a mere indiscriminate herd of YOUS? To this period the memory of man, at least, runneth not back, and the oldest historical representations open with a personal nomenclature somewhat of the nature of the sobriquet or nickname—a single name freely designating some idiosyncrasy of the individual. A broad, free, spontaneous method was this—seizing some emphatic piece of personnel, and making it the symbol of the man. Hercules, Ulysses, Diogenes, Socrates, Isaac, Jacob are instances from Greek and Hebrew nomenclature.

An advance on this primitive nomenclature was the assumption of the name of one's *sire* in addition to his own proper name, as Melchi ben Addi—Melchi, son of Addi; Ικαρος του Δαιδαλου—Icarus, son of Dædalus. Additional definiteness was gained by the annexation of an epithet indicative of his country or some personal or social peculiarity, as Herodotus *of Halicarnassus;* Diogenes *the Cynic;* Alexander *the Great.*

But the perfection of personal nomenclature was the introduction of the Surname proper—a name superadded to the first or Christian name, to indicate the family to which the individual bearing it belongs. Du Cange asserts that Surnames were at first written "not in a direct line *after* the Christian name, but *above* it, between the lines"—and so, literally, *supra-nomina* or *over*-names. English hereditary Surnames were among the fruits of that mighty social revolution that came with the Norman conquest. As says the great Camden, "About the year of our Lord 1000, (that we may not minute out the time) surnames became to be taken up in France; and in England about the time of the Conquest, or else a very little before, under King Edward the Confessor, who was all Frenchified. This will seeme strange to some Englishmen and Scottishmen, whiche, like the Arcadians, thinke their surnames as antient as the moon, or at least to reach many an age beyond the Conquest. But they which thinke it most strange (I speake under correction), I doubt they will hardly finde any surname which descended to posterity before that time: neither have they seene (I feare) any deede or donation before the Conquest but subsigned with crosses and single names without surnames, in this manner: + Ego Eadredus confirmaui. + Ego Edmundus corroboraui. + Ego Sigarius conclusi," etc.

Lower makes a classification of English surnames

as originating in Locality, Occupations, Dignities, Physical and Mental Qualities, Natural Objects, Social Relations, Contempt, Virtues and Vices, Historical Events, Oaths and Exclamations, Puns, Whimsicalities, etc. I can but select a few typical examples.

Local Surnames. This is a copious source of names, every feature in Geography having fossilized into numerous personal appellations. BURNS, BRYDGES (Scotch BRIGGS), BROOKS, CRAGGS, the CHASE (or forest), the FIELD, FOLD and FOREST, the GRANGE, GROVE, HILL and HOUSE, the HOLMES (meadow surrounded by water), KNOWLES (top of a hill), and LOWNDES (or lawns), MARSH, MILL, MOSS and MOUNTAIN, PARK, PITT, POOLE, and SANDS, the STREET, SPIRE, TREE and TOWER, and finally every quarter, NORTH, SOUTH, EAST and WEST have contributed to swell the list.

Occupations and Pursuits. In this marshaling of Names with reference to their sources, next in number to the local contributions are the contributions from Occupations and Pursuits. These became a natural resort for nomenclature with the advance of the arts. "PARSONS and PRIESTS met with CHURCHES and PARISHES and DYERS bound to COFFINS, while GRAVES yawned before both; BREWER sent out BEERS, and FISHER brought in EELS; and, in short, every body had the *name* of doing something in the way of his trade."

But whence came all the SMITHS? Momentous question! An acceptable enough answer is contained in this old rhyme which Verstegan quotes as current in his time:

> "From whence comes *Smith*, all be he Knight or Squyre,
> But from the *Smith* that *forgeth* at the fyre?"

SMITH, then, is originally one who *smitheth*—Smi(te)th. But as the Saxon verb *smitan* was applied to workers in wood as well as to those in metal, SMITH meant a *smiter* in general, including wheelwrights, carpenters, masons, etc. And hence the frequency of the name.

Leaving the Smiths we have the MILLERS, MASONS, CARPENTERS, BAKERS, GOLDSMITHS, SHEPHERDS, BUTLERS, BUTCHERS, CARTERS, COOPERS, COLLIERS, LAWYERS, TAYLORS, etc. JENNER is an old form of *joiner;* WEBSTER is properly the feminine of *weaver.* The associations of field-sports have left us HUNTERS, FOWLERS, FISHERS, FALCONERS, HAWKERS, ARROWSMITHS and FLETCHERS (French *flèche,* an arrow), which is Norman for the same. But what do you say of HOPPERS, SKIPPERS and JUMPERS?

And then, Offices and Dignities have left us a large nominal legacy—from EMPEROR and KING, through PRINCES, EARLES and LORDS, down to the plain YEOMAN and SQUIRE. The Church has given us POPES, BISHOPS, PARSONS, PRIESTS and CLARKS (CLARKES). The State has given us, *entre autres*, CHANCELLORS, MAYORS and REEVES. As for SPENCER, it is simply *Le Despencer*, the *dispenser;* CHALMERS (*Chambers*) is primarily *De la Chambre* the *Chamberlain;* and FRANKLIN records a piece of primitive English socialism—being etymologically just a *freeholder*. Chaucer, in the Prologue to the Canterbury Tales, has a lively picture of the Franklin, which begins after this wise:

"A FRANKELEIN was in this compagnie
White was his berd, as is the dayesie.
Of his complexion he was sanguin," etc.

PILGRIM and PALMER! The crusades rise at the names!—the PILGRIMS on their way to the Holy Land, the PALMERS with their *palm-branches* in their hands.*

"His sandals were with travel tore,
Staff, budget, bottle, scrip he wore;

* Lower on Surnames.

The faded *palm-branch* in his hand
Shewed *pilgrim* from the Holy Land."

Marmion.

Personnel. A fruitful source of nominal roots are Personal and Mental Qualities. How easy for sobriquets to arise from some external or internal idiosyncrasy, as BLACK, BROWN, WHITE (WHITMAN), GREY; or he was a LONGMAN or a LONGFELLOW or STRONG or SMALL or SWIFT or STOUT. REED, READ or REID, are all variations of RED. MEEK, NOBLE and STERNE, too, had doubtless once a positive metaphysical significance. GIFFORD is one given to *giving* (Saxon *Gifan*, to give). SWEET, FREEMAN, GOODENOUGH! DOOLITTLE contains a sad confession. And what shall we say to Mr. DRINKWATER? Fantastic enough, certainly. But have not the French also their BOILEAU? And the apotheosis of all the virtues appears in PEACE, HOPE, JOY, MERCY, BLISS!

Natural Objects. Nature, too, has been harried for appellations. Descending from SUN and STARS, we take in the whole animal world, as (quadrupeds) LYON, BUCK, HART, LAMB, HOGG (akin to BACON), BULLOCK; (birds) HERON, CRANE, JAY, ROOKE; (fishes) PIKE, CRABBE, HERRING; (insects) WASP, FLY, etc. The vegetable world comes in for its share

—MYRTLE, SAGE, PEPPER, PEASE, LEMON and PEEL. Nor has the mineral kingdom escaped—as STONE, FLINT, STEELE, JEWELL!

Oddities. Lower, under this head, gives a curious list of odd names that probably arose from sobriquets formerly applied to the individuals. Among these are appellations derived from parts of the human body, as HEAD, BONES, BACK, HEART, TOE, HEELE, SOLE; or from coins, as FARTHING, PENNY, MONEYPENNY; or from the weather, as FROST, SNOW, HAIL; or numbers, as SIX, FORTYE, ONCE, TWICE. Have Messrs. PHYSIC and COFFIN any necessary kinship? And what is one to say of such forms as these but that they are pure nicknames: CROOKSHANKS, LONGSHANKS, GOSLING, TREE, BLOOD, DEATH!

But the farthest reaches of nominal fancies are to be found in the grotesque Christian names which the Puritans, during the Sixteenth and Seventeenth Centuries, were fond of giving themselves. "Sometimes," says Hume, "a whole godly sentence was adopted as a name;" and he quotes the names of a Sussex jury, that runs after this wise:

Stand-fast-on-high Stringer of Crowhurst,
More-fruite Fowler of East-Hadley,
Kill-sin Pimple of Witham,
Fight-the-good-fight-of-faith White of Ewen, etc.

Ben Jonson, in *Bartholemew Fair*, thus throws his thought into Dialogue:

Q. His Christen-name is Zeal-of-the-Land.

L. Yes, Sir, Zeal-of-the-Land Busy.

W. How! What a name's there!

L. O, they have all such names, Sir; he was witness for Winbere (they will not be called God-fathers) and named her Win-the-fight: you thought her name had been Winnifred, did you not?

W. I did indeed.

L. He would ha' thought himself a stark reprobate if it had.

But the most extraordinary one I have yet met with is the following—itself a perfect catechism *in petto:* If-Christ-had-not-died-for-thee-thou-had'st-been-damned Dobson!

A very evident mode of forming names of persons would be to join the father's—the *sire's name*—to that of the child, connecting them by some word to indicate the relationship. Thus the Scotch Highlanders have their *Mac*—'MACDONALD,' for instance—or as we would have it, 'DONALD*son*' (i.e. *Donald's son*). So the Normans have their *Fitz*—supposed to be just a corruption of *fils* (filius—a *son*); the Irish their *O'*; the Russians their *Witz;* the Poles their *Sky*—

'PETERSON,' for instance, being with them, 'PETROWSKY;' and the Welsh their *Ap*—which, however, we are not always very careful to preserve—David ap Howel (i.e. David, son of Howel) appearing simply as David Powell, and John ap Richard, as the plain John Pritchard.

The Welsh affectation of joining together the names of a score or two of ancestors (connecting them by their endless 'APS') has given rise to more banter and pleasantry than we could conveniently notice Tim Bobbin has some curiosities in this way. It was not unusual, a century or two back, to hear of such combinations as Evan-ap-Griffth-ap-David-ap-Jenkin; and some wag, in the way of burlesque, described *cheese* as being

"Adam's own cousin-german by its birth,
Ap-Curds-ap-Milk-ap-Cow-ap-Grass-ap-Earth."

Such names as these, declares Lower, cast the Dutch *Inkvervankodsdorspanckinkadrachdern* quite into the shade!

Our Saxon names are often profoundly significant. 'ALFRED,' for instance, is *All peace;* 'BERNARD' is *Bearen* (or Bear's) *heart;* 'EDGAR' is Ead-gard—one who *guards* his (ead) oath—a troth-keeper; 'ED-

WARD' is the same as Edgar (*ward=guard*); 'GOODWIN' is a *Good-win*—who *wins goods*, or wealth: so 'ROBERT' is said to signify one *disposed to rest*—and the account which Verstegan gives of the origin of the name 'WILLIAM' is very curious: He says that in the wars between the Germans and Romans, the Roman officers were in the habit of wearing gilded head-pieces; and whenever a German soldier killed a Roman officer, this gilded head-piece was put on the soldier's head, so that he forthwith became a *Gild-helm* (a Golden helmet)—what the Latins call *Guilielmus*, the French *Guillaume*, and we 'WILLIAM.'

The name of the various trades and professions might form a curiously interesting subject for investigation under this same head. A 'CLOTHIER,' for instance, is very evidently one who deals in *cloth* or *clothes*—a 'DRAPER,' as we say, which is just 'clothier' in French—*drap* being their word for *cloth*. So, a 'TAILOR' is one whose business it is to—*tailler*—to *cut out* garments; but, not only to cut them out, but also to *sew them together*—a realization obtained by 'COSIER,' which Shakespeare, in the *Twelfth Night*, uses, though we have not retained the term. A 'FARRIER,' again, is plainly one who works in—*ferrum*—iron—*shoeing* a horse being expressed both in French and Italian by *ironing* a horse; while a 'CURRIER' finds his employment in—cuir—*leather*, and a 'SEXTON is just a *sacristan*.

Pegge says—whether right or wrong—that 'APOTHECARY' (the old *potecary*) is originally a *boticario*—i.e., one who has a *shop*, what we would call a 'STATIONER' (only that *that* has acquired a *special* signification), in opposition to a 'PEDLER'—who is, of course, continually trudging along *on his feet*—pedes. A 'BUTCHER' is doubtless just the French *boucher*—a form which, by the way, we find in old literature. Thus the "beastly Skelton" says:

> "For drede of the *Boucher's* dog
> Wold worry them like a hog."

And a 'GROCER' rather boastingly declares that he deals only *in gross*. Johnson, indeed, recommended that the word be spelled *grosser**—which has certainly

* Our age is no respecter of *letters*. In our retrenchment and amendment we deal with them just as if *they* had no feeling on the subject. Once, we know, Orthography was a more serious affair; for "Worthy" Fuller tells us of a clerk in the culinary department of the royal household, who narrowly escaped condign punishment for spelling *C*inapi as *S*inapi.

Church History, Book IV. p. 156.

the warrant of etymology. This is but a hint of an immense theme.

The theory of nomenclature finally ascends into the æsthetical realm—vast and hitherto all but unexplored domain. The necessities of Literary Art—especially as expressed in the drama and novel—require the creation of ideal Names. And often high and highest art is displayed in the workings of creative Imagination on nominal emblems for these avatars of the mind. The masters of the modern Novel all work, consciously or unconsciously, on the problem of Names. I know books that suggest ideal pedigrees, a new heraldry of the mind, and carry farther out the boundaries of Metaphysics.

To Modern times and to America, too, the thought of Naming presents itself. Once, we know, every name was significant. There have been seasons, in the elder ages, of flood-tides in the creative faculties, when Nature disclosed her secret thought and gave it to man to name her—when to mountain and stream, field and flood were added names that are poems. Why should not we, too, come into this Orphic secret? Why should we masquerade in the old costume? Imperative is the demand for a fresh, free, appropriate nomenclature for American Geography,

Inventions, Contributions, Personalities. Already the new needs make the old perfections meagre and inadequate. To you, Poets and Builders, sublime invitations! To quarry and to build in the new architectures of humanity.

RAMBLE TENTH.

SYNONYMS AND THEIR SUGGESTIONS.

"All languages tend to clear themselves of synonyms as intellectual culture advances—the superfluous words being taken up and appropriated by new shades and combinations of thought evolved in the progress of society."

DE QUINCEY.

AN adequate treatment of English Synonyms is still a desideratum. Crabbe's work was written before Philology became a science, and the little volume edited by Archbishop Whately clean skips etymology and all its seminal suggestions. Mr. Taylor ("English Synonyms Discriminated") commands the etymologic method, and has furnished an important contribution to Synonymy: but his work is not at all proportioned to the copiousness of our language. Of much profounder philosophic significance is the *The-*

*saurus** of Mr. Roget, who has given us a metaphysical classification of Thoughts and Things with their corresponding Verbal Symbols—"furnishing on every topic a copious store of words and phrases, adapted to express all the recognizable shades and modifications of the general idea under which those words and phrases are arranged." These various works are all useful auxiliaries; but I return to the assertion with which I set out, that an adequate treatment of this subject is still something to be desired. A great Synonymy, after the modern Philologic Methods, would be a most important contribution to the Philosophy of the English language. Much is in the subject; much grows out of it.

But are there any such words as synonyms? Of absolutely equivalent, absolutely equipollent expressions there are necessarily few. Not but that terms between which exists a certain Algebraic equality are to be found: the number is small, however, and constantly diminishing. It is the tendency of an advancing culture—of an expansion of the horizon of thoughts and things—to eliminate synonyms by separating kindred terms and stamping each respectively

* Thesaurus of English Words and Phrases, Classified and Arranged so as to Facilitate the Expression of Ideas and Assist in Literary Composition. London, 1852.

with the seal and superscription of an intellectual individuality. Of synonymous words we shall then have to say, that they are such as, bearing general and generic resemblances, have yet specific differences, and a color and contour of their own.

The causes of the growth of Synonyms lie deep in the roots of a nation's life and language. Relations, external and internal, act—amalgamation of races, literary influence and action of other nations, the prominent elements of national civilization, with other and subtler causes. With a people of active imagination there is always a tendency to drape the crowning facts and factors of its life with a copious richness of expressive forms. And it is significant to notice the manner in which even individual elements in a nation's civilization have been affected with verbal powers. In the era of chivalry there was a host of expressions to render the idea of *horse.* In Sanscrit, the language of Hindostàn, where the *elephant* plays a part as important as the horse among ourselves, words abound to designate this pachyderm. Sometimes it is denominated the 'twice-drinking animal,' sometimes as 'he who has two teeth,' sometimes as 'the animal with the proboscis.'* This is still

* Alfred Maury.

more strikingly manifest in the Arabic, which is said to have the enormous multitude of several hundred words for the 'ship of the desert.'

These divers influences have all acted on the English Speech. Complex in its organism as no language is, it inherits all that antiquity conceived and freely augments and enriches itself with importations from the modern idioms. Born thus of the marriage of several stocks and tongues, a copious equivalence runs through the English language, and it frequently depends on a writer's choice whether his diction shall bear the features of this or that branch of his linguistic ancestry.

Of this hospitality of our language numerous illustrations present themselves. Thus the good strong Saxon 'TRICK' has always been a living part of our speech, expressing a sly fraud: but, not content with this single symbol, early in the literary history of our language a double inoculation of words from the classics took place—the Greek contributing 'STRATAGEM' (*stratagema*), the Latin 'ARTIFICE' (*artificium*). Nor is this all. With the study of Italian literature, during the reign of James I., 'DEVICE' was introduced; and a still farther importation was made, under the writers of Charles II.—with whom a French renaissance took place—of the term 'FINESSE.'

Thus it is that the English language has enriched itself from a five-fold source with words for the expression of a single general idea. And here precisely it is that the constant law of *Desynonymizing*, as Coleridge expressively terms it, comes into play, and a gradual divergence, a gradual individualizing of each term takes place: and so it is that, in the final assortment, while 'TRICK' continues its general, social significance, 'ARTIFICE' carries with it rather the meaning of a mechanical contrivance, 'STRATAGEM' a military feint; 'DEVICE' was gradually exported into heraldry, "describing the hieroglyph by means of which the name of a chieftain is enigmatically written on his shield," while 'FINESSE'—which has the French charm of vagueness—is gradually assuming the sense of intellectual subtlety. Take another illustration. 'Blast,' 'Gale,' 'Gust,' 'Storm,' 'Tempest,' 'Hurricane.' Here are six words all expressive of violent atmospheric phenomena, and which, coming from various linguistic sources, have all been naturalized in our language and have elaborated for themselves a distinctive individuality. It is only, however, the clue of etymology that discloses the proper shape and shade belonging to each of these terms. And it is instructive to note what subtle facts are exposed by the opening up of the interior import of these word-histories. For 'GUST' and 'STORM' are of Northern origin (Danish and Icelandic in their connections), and suggest the phenomena of northern climates—'gust' carrying with it the fitful *gush* of the wind; and 'storm' being more violent, more complex—the *stir*, namely, of the atmospheric elements; fierce rapid meteorologic commotion, throwing air and earth and ocean into elemental contest, with darkness, perchance, and destruction and hail and snow. 'TEMPEST' is of southern origin and describes the sort of storm common in warm countries, where quite a-*time*-of-it (*tempestas*, *tempus*, time) is of frequent occurrence, wind accompanied with rain and lightenings and thunder. 'HURRICANE' though of Spanish or French origin (Spanish *huracan;* French *ouragan*) has yet a historical and geographical connection with the storm-phenomena of the West Indies and the Caribean Sea; and hence is in its very nature peculiarly fitted to typify tropical and summer storms. As I am on the vocabulary of tempests, it occurs to me to mention an additional synonym to the preceding, and which did not come into my mind when writing the above. I refer to the word 'TORNADO.' And here, too, the magic wand of Etymology is of potent service. For is it not patent that the connection of this term with the verb to *turn* (Spanish and Portuguese *tornada*, a turning round) is suggestive of precisely the element that most eminently characterizes these oriental tempests—the *whirling* motion, the *whirlwind*, namely?

But let me enter into the subject of Synonyms with somewhat more of system. And in this estimation of the influences that have acted on the growth of Synonyms we shall follow the line of history if we notice such correlative expressions as arose from the inoculation, early in the history of our language, of the large Norman element that came with the Norman Conquest. Such correlatives are very numerous. And it is a significant fact that the antagonism that long subsisted between the Saxon and Norman races is vividly mirrored in our language. For presently a fierce hostility arose between the contending native and foreign terms, and Saxon and Norman verbs and substantives waged a war as bitter as that recently carried on by Saxon and Norman men.

Various of course were the fortunes of the day. At times, the Gallicism clean overpowered and supplanted the Saxonism; at others, the French word had to yield before the imperious home-instinct. Now a Saxon noun fell into disuse, a Norman substitute taking its place, and only the *adjective* remaining as a reminiscence of the old vocable; anon, both words were retained, some compromise being struck between them—the Saxon, perchance, crystallizing around the homelier, heartier nucleus of meaning; the Gallicism employed in the more courtly, more *recherché* signification.

And first, of such duplicates the native form of which the French finally succeeded in eliminating. The Saxon term for a tiller of the ground was *earthling*—a word of sweet and tender beauty, which I cannot but wish had been retained—gave place to the Norman 'FARMER'—*fermier;* while *earthling* has completely lost all its old vitality and been pressed into the moral service. Relations, social and political, coming under the control of the invaders, the new regime made itself powerfully and practically felt in the dealings of the law, of which here is an illustration. To express the legal union of the sexes the Normans imposed on the conquered Saxon their word 'MARRIAGE,' which is just the getting of a *mari* or husband (getting a *man*, as the Scotch say)—supplanting thus the native expression, *gyfta* (a *giving away*). This, though, is but the external, the convention part: the heart of the matter continued still to be expressed by the Saxon 'WEDDING,' an expressive word, originating in *wed*, a pledge, a covenant. And here are some native words every vestige of which has disappeared from our speech. *Month-sick* has been supplanted by 'LUNATIC,' *behodun* by 'COMMANDMENT,' *anweald* by 'AUTHORITY,' *agilt* by 'RECOMPENSE,' and *afgodnes* by 'IDOLATRY.'

Or again, there occurs an outcropping of the old form, as primary strata shoot up through the walls of the world. *Bead* is no longer a living English word, having given place to 'PRAYER' (French *prière*): and yet we have reminiscences thereof in the *beads*, on which the Catholic counts his *prayers;* in the *bead-roll* (*bede-roll*) which was the *roll* or list of persons to be *prayed* for, and in the memory of the old *beadsman*, who was to bless and pray, dropping his *beads*, and saying

"Stranger go! Heaven be thy guide."

Burns.

'STEWARD' seems to have undergone quite a degeneracy. For the composition of the word would imply that he was originally the *stede-ward* (sted-ward, ste(d)ward = *steward**) the *ward*, *guard* or keeper in the *stead* or place of another—a meaning which was afterwards covered by the French 'LIEUTENANT:' and then it was that the declension of *steward* began,

* In regard to *steward* Webster says, "the meaning of the first syllable is not evident!" I can't imagine anything more evident. But he was misled, as so frequently, by Johnson.

sinking down into a mere *butler* or *bottle*-er! 'HEADY' and 'TESTY' (French *teste*, *tête*, the head) are etymologically entirely coincident, and yet they soon began to diverge in meaning, while 'HEADY' is now all but obsolete. Or consider this duplicate—to 'whiten' and to 'blanch,' the first of the native stock, the latter of the Norman importation (*blanchir*, *blanc*, white). Here, too, the etymologic coincidence is perfect. It was not long, however, before they gradually began to fall apart—to *whiten* meaning to superinduce a white color, whereas *blanch* implies the withdrawal of some coloring matter, which concealed the natural color. Similar is the duplicity that was found between 'THOUGHTFUL' (Saxon) and 'PENSIVE' (French): in time, however, the national instinct appropriated the latter term to symbolize the sentimental side of the quality—'PENSIVE' superinducing on *thoughtfulness* an element of soft *sadness*. The Norman never could usurp the Saxon's *home* and *hearth*, although he did succeed in leaving his impress on many a stately 'mansion;' and yet most effectually did he invade the *manners* and *customs* of our ancestors, introducing his own 'modes' and 'fashions' —putting 'bonnets'—which is French every letter of it—on women's heads, although he never managed to take the 'hats' (Saxon *hæt*) and 'caps' (Saxon *cæppe*) from off men; dressing ladies out in 'frocks' (French *froc*), and gentlemen in 'coats' (French *cotte*); throwing 'shawls' over the shoulders of the one sex and 'surtouts' on the backs of the other, and transforming the home-spun 'bræcs' into the more elegant 'pantaloons!'

But in this survey of Synonyms, a further retrospect is required. And such were the causes that worked in the development of the English language that, besides these French correlatives, it presents manifold duplicates, Saxon and Latin, and many triplicates, Saxon, Latin, and Greek—introduced at a later day when the suns of classic language, culture and thought came with their vernal and fecundating influence over the nascent English speech. How many such duplicates as these do we have:

Saxon.	*Latin.*
FREEDOM	LIBERTY
FEAR	TERROR
MEAT	VICTUALS
DALE	VALE
GUESS	CONJECTURE
WEARINESS	LASSITUDE
FATHERLY	PATERNAL
RICH	OPULENT

Saxon.	*Latin.*
WHOLE	ENTIRE
HIDDEN	OCCULT
SOUR	ACID
TAME	GENTLE
HATE	ABHOR
HELP	ASSIST
DIE	EXPIRE
BETTER	MELIORATE
LESSEN	DIMINISH
TRUST	CREDIT

These new factors coming in to do their work in the growth of our tongue, the result was that many a significant combination arose. And first, we find triplicates in which a Saxon, French, and Latin term stood side by side, each severally coming gradually to assert and assume a sphere of its own. Thus from the three roots *country* (Saxon), *pays* (French), and *rus* (Latin)—three synonymous roots from as many distinct sources—arise 'COUNTRYMAN,' 'PEASANT,' and 'RUSTIC.' 'FORESIGHT' comes to us a native-bred home-word: with the Norman inoculation came 'PRUDENCE,' etymologically an exact synonym of the foregoing: but, not satisfied with this duality, writers in the course of time went back to the Roman idiom and imported thence 'PROVIDENCE,' whereof 'PRU-

DENCE' is simply the French form. King=*roy* (French)=*rex* (Latin): 'Kingly'='royal'='regal.' And here are a few additional triplets that come under this same category: 'bold,' 'brave,' 'intrepid' —'wrath,' 'rage,' 'ire'—'leave,' 'abandon,' 'desert' —'bear,' 'support,' 'tolerate'—'east,' 'levant,' 'orient'—'lust,' 'desire,' 'cupidity—'chosen, 'recherché,' 'elegant' ('select').

But I must advance, in the cozenage of words, to importations made at once from Latin and Greek. And perhaps the briefest way will be for me to tabulate a handful or so out of the multitudes of these correlatives.

Saxon.	*Latin.*	*Greek.*
STARRY	SIDERIAL	ASTRAL
SPEECH	LANGUAGE	DIALECT
SAW	PROVERB	APHORISM
WAYWARD	ERRATIC	ECCENTRIC
WELL-BRED	AFFABLE	POLITE
AIM	VIEW	SCOPE
GUESS	CONJECTURE	HYPOTHESIS
CURSE	MALEDICTION	ANATHEMA
STRESS	ACCENT	EMPHASIS
FOE	OPPONENT	ANTAGONIST
TALE	NOVEL	STORY
PITHY	CONCISE	LACONIC

I invite to an exploration of these and similar

groups—many a curious fact or fancy will they reveal. Take the triplet 'foe'—'opponent'—'antagonist,' for example. The Saxon 'FOE,' has its connections in the Teutonic verbs *feon*, *fian*,* to hate, and means (any one) *hated*—and hence is of these terms the one that carries with it the burden of the most active hostility; 'OPPONENT,' indeed, is one who is *pitted against* (*ob* and *pono*) another, while 'ANTAGONIST' has its origin in the *antagonistes* of the Grecian games. Or consider this group—'wayward,' 'erratic,' 'eccentric:' on what a vivid perception of character do they rest. 'WAYWARD' is just *away*-ward—the tendency to be off and away—an image perfectly realized by 'ERRATIC,' which is the being given to *erring*, or wandering—

> "The extravagant and *erring* spirit hies
> To his confines."
>
> *Hamlet.*

'ECCENTRIC' is an importation from geometry, typifying the tendency to depart from the *centre*—"flying off in a tangent" from the centred round of customary thinkings and actings. Or explore the suggestions in this group—'tale,' 'novel,' 'story.' 'TALE' has its

* 'FIEND' is the present participle of this verb, and signifies the *hater*. The interjections 'FIE' 'FOH' and 'FAUGH' have all a like genesis.

roots in the verb to *tell*, and hence is properly confined to a short narrative within the compass of conversational convenience, and fitted to amuse the hearer; 'STORY,' however, in its very origin professes to be true (*historia*), while the primary characteristic of the 'NOVEL' is that it have *novelty*.* Finally, of the group 'pithy,' 'concise,' and 'laconic;' 'PITHY' claims to shut up in a small compass much *pith*, much of the spine and spirit of the matter under consideration; while 'CONCISE' (*concisus*, cut off) prunes and lops off all verbal excess and redundancy, and 'LACONIC' is after the fashion of the *Lacones* or men of Laconia—the Spartans—a grave, brief, sententious race.

Having taken this historical coup-d'œil of Synonyms, it may be permitted us to enter into the subject with somewhat more of freedom. It is curious to observe how, in the final assortment of correlative terms, the national instinct wrought on each, and what is the fate that has befallen these several analogues—how the degrees of praise and blame, of merit and demerit have varied with the pulsings of the popular heart. Of this action such words as 'womanly'—'feminine;' 'boyish'—'puerile;' 'lively'—'vital;' 'friendly'—'amical,' etc., afford illustrations. As far

* Taylor: Synonyms Discriminated.

as composition goes, 'WOMANLY' and 'FEMININE' are entirely coincident and correspondent: and yet see how the formative popular energy has wrought on these words. For who does not perceive that there is something infinitely loving in 'WOMANLY,' that 'FEMININE' (which merely denotes that which pertains to woman *as the opposite sex*—and for which *womanish* was formerly employed) can lay no claim to? Chaucer's beautiful lines come in here with expressive significance:

> "I see wel that ye have on my distresse
> Compassion, my faire Canese,
> Of veray* *womanly* benignitie,
> That nature in your principles hath set."
>
> *The Squieres Tale.*

On the other hand, a passage from Milton will set 'FEMININE' in almost too clear a light.

> "Yet the fourth time when mustering all her wiles,
> With blandisht parlies, *feminine* assaults,
> Tongue-batteries, she surceased not day nor night
> To storm me overwatched and wearied out."
>
> *Samson Agonistes.*

'CHILDLIKE' is a very beautiful and ingenuous

* What we write *very;* 'VERY' is, therefore, just *truly—vrai.*

term, and yet 'INFANTINE' or 'INFANTILE,' albeit just the Latin therefor, have none of its charming simplicity—nay, they are altogether 'childish,' although it may not be unworthy of note that even *it* had formerly precisely the meaning of 'childlike,' as in the following:

"Charitie is a *childish* thing, as holi churche wittnesseth *nisi efficiamini sicut parvuli.*

Piers Ploughman, p. 280.

There is nothing offensive about 'BOYISH,' and yet who would wish to be charged with being 'PUERILE,' either in word or deed? Dryden introduced 'BOYISM,' but I know not that it survived him. It is instructive to observe how the balance of Compensation in time equalizes and adjusts every thing: for even 'PUERILE' had once nothing contemptuous about it, but was, in fact, precisely analogous to our present acceptation of 'BOYISH.' An instance of this from Anthony-à-Wood suggests itself:

"Franciscus Junius was born at Heidelberg a famous city and university of Germany an. 1589, educated in *puerile* learning at Leyden," etc.

Athenæ Oxon.

Compare the home-bred 'LIVELY' with the imported 'VITAL.' Is there not something more in 'LIVELY' than the mere possession of *vitality*—a something of quickness and vivacity superadded thereto which 'VITAL' possesses not, and which for ever prevents them from coalescing? 'FRIENDLY,' too—can it be because it is a tone of our old mother tongue?—seems to wear an infinitely more winning smile, and an infinitely warmer heart than does the more stately 'AMICAL,' or the somewhat frigid 'AMICABLE.'

But, if our strong Saxonisms sometimes have the advantage over their high-born Southern sisters, the reverse is oft times the case: the Omnipresent, Omnipotent Law of Compensation which balances granules and gravitation here also makes itself felt, and unerringly adjusts the terms of the great linguistic equation. 'BLOODY' and 'SANGUINE' afford an illustration to the point. For though from analogous roots (*sanguis* = *blood*)—yet has the Latin by far the milder meaning—implying, at present, rather that expectant, confiding disposition that is generally found in union with an ardent temperament and a copious flow of *blood*. Chapman, however, frequently employs it as synonymous with bloody. As here:

"Sharpe axes, turbils, two-hand swords, and spears
with two heads borne,

Were then the weapons: faire short swords with
sanguine hilts still worn,
Had use in like sort." *Iliad, XV.**

'WORLDLY' and 'EARTHLY' have clustered much of their meaning round ethical pivots—worldly implying the being too much attached to the world—to

"This *earthly* load
Of death called life:"

whereas 'MUNDANE' and 'TERRESTRIAL' (and 'EARTHY,' too,) have to a much greater extent preserved their merely expletive and definitive acceptation.

This principle, indeed, we find running through a very prolific class of synonyms: the Saxon adjective being the homely, hearty, common word—with, perchance, a poetic or sentimental sense superadded thereto: while the Latin remains literal—rigid and scientific. Instances innumerable might be adduced in illustration. 'HEARTY' may be no more than 'cordial,' yet is it much more than 'cardiac;' while what is quite 'salutary' may not always be very 'healthy.' There is poetry in 'sunny' and 'starry'

* But the heroic translator of the old blind Bard is frequently very erratic in his use of words—almost always employing them in their literal, *classic* sense. Thus for the word in its above acceptation, we now use 'SANGUINARY.'

and 'fiery' and 'icy' and 'glassy,' but not an atom can be extracted from 'solar' or 'stellar' ('astral,' 'sidereal,' etc.) or 'igneous' or 'glacial' or vitreous'—the corresponding adjectives of Latin origin. 'Hairy' cannot be defined by 'capillary,' nor 'handy' by 'manual,' while 'doggish' ('dogged,' etc.) has an innate *snappish* and cynic force that is not responded to by 'canine.' No poet would hesitate, as to beauty and expressiveness, between 'nightly' and 'nocturnal,' or between 'wintry' and 'brumal,' even though he might not remember that our Saxon forefathers were wont to count time by nights, and the years of their life-time by winters.* It is not, however, always the case that the Latin retains the literal, while the Saxon receives the metaphorical application. Thus 'woody' is nearer the literal truth than is 'sylvan'—even though *it* has its root in the Roman *forest* (*sylva*).

It frequently happens, too, that the presence of these various factors in our language has made strange work with the parts of speech. And significant among these results is the existence of numerous couplets, whereof the substantive is a Saxonism, the adjective

* Traces of this crop out in our terms *se'night* and *fortnight*, i..e *seven* nights; *fourteen* nights (hence).

a classicism. Thus though 'MIND' is a primitive Saxon vocable, the English genius never succeeded in elaborating for itself a term expressive of *having relation to the mind:* straightway it was compelled to have recourse to the Latin, importing thence, for that purpose, the word 'MENTAL' (*mens*, mind)—a word well fitted for adjective expression. So, *being* was forced to go forth and find abstract realization in 'ESSENTIAL;' *thing* in 'REAL;' *reason* in 'RATIONAL;' *root* in 'RADICAL;' *kind* in 'GENERAL,' and *will* in 'VOLUNTARY.' Would it be to divide too nicely to say that the omnipresent laws of Race work here too: and that the fact of the English speech never having been able to attain to free intellectual abstractions, from roots within itself, runs parallel with that powerful practicality and realism that has always so markedly characterized the English stock. Let me illustrate somewhat more at length. *Ground* is a good strong nervous word; and yet we are fain to go to the Latin, take their corresponding word—*humus*—convert it into an adjective (*humilis*), put it through the French crucible, and then inoculate it on our language, looking very 'HUMBLE' indeed. All our senses have gone the same way. 'Twould be vulgar to use the 'NOSE' for 'SMELLING,' but the 'NASAL' organ for 'OLFACTORY' purposes! 'HEARING' transforms itself into 'AUDITORY,' and I know not how we could otherwise express '*auricular* confession.' Yet we would not receive 'eye-proof,' but '*ocular* demonstration,' while for adjectives we must travel to Greece and Rome—stealing away 'OPTIC' and 'VISUAL.' Shall we say '*tasty?*' A milliner, as Coleridge remarks, might! What then? Why, 'GUSTATORY,' 'ÆSTHETIC,' or what not. Science, too, with its mighty modern strides, has been compelled to seek symbols in these antique fountains. Thus *tooth* finds a correlative in 'dental;' *lungs* in 'pulmonary;' *lip* in 'labial;' *navel* in 'umbilical;' *marrow* in 'medullary;' *elbow* in 'cubital;' *breast* in 'pectoral;' *foot* in 'pedal;' *birth* in 'natal;' *cat* in 'feline;' *calf* in 'feline;' *cow* in 'vaccine;' *eagle* in 'aquiline;' *horse* in 'equine;' *house* in 'domestic.' So the very

Simple.		*Complex.*
MEAL	appears as very	FARINACEOUS
SWEAT		SUDORIFIC
SLEEP		SOPORIFEROUS
FEAR		TIMOROUS
THANKS		GRATUITOUS
HELP		AUXILIARY
HIRE		MERCENARY
SEA		MARITIME
LEAP		DESULTORY
NOISE		OBSTREPEROUS
ALMS		ELEEMOSYNARY!

Donner and Blitzen! Seven syllables out of one! But let Horne Tooke give us the why and the wherefore.

"With the Christian religion were very early introduced to our ancestors the Greek words, *Church*, *Parish*, *People*, *Alms*: which they corrupted and used as substantives, a long time before they wanted them in an *adjectived* state. When the latter time arrived, they were incapable of *adjectiving* these words themselves, and were therefore forced to seek them in the original language. Hence the Adjectives are not so corrupt as the Substantives. And hence the strange appearance of *Eleemosynary*, a word of seven syllables, as the Adjective of the monosyllable *Alms*; which itself became such by successive corruptions of ELEEMOSUNE long before its Adjective was required: having successively exhibited itself as *Almosine*, *Almosie*, *Almose*, *Almes*, and finally *Alms*; whilst in the French language it appeared as *Almosine*, *Almosne*, *Aumosne*, *Aumône*."*

The rounds that words make are indeed often curiously erratic. Thus the Latin adjective *salvus* becomes transformed into the French *sauf*, whence it comes to us in the shape of 'SAFE,' from this we form, also, 'SAFETY.' But an analogous word being found

* Diversions of Purley, p. 639.

necessary for a spiritual application, we went back again to the Latin and transferred their *salvatio* into our 'SALVATION:' 'SALVATION' and 'SAFETY' are therefore, properly, one word—being differenced only by the process of derivation.

And, by the way, it is instructive to observe the very widely divergent words that we frequently find formed from one root. So widely divergent that they oftentimes appear to have no connection with each other; and it is only the Ariadne-thread of Etymology that gives us a clue through the labyrinth of verbal forms. The words 'PITY' and 'PIETY' afford an instructive example. These emotions the Spanish, Portuguese, Italian and Latin languages all unite in expressing by one and the same term. The Latin furnishes the radix from which all the others spring. For 'PIETAS' implies that state of feeling which causes us to act rightly both towards the gods and towards men; and since tenderness and compassion are prime elements in this beautiful passion, there was no necessity felt for separating them by diverse terms. Nor was it until the French made the unnatural divorce (and the English here, as in so many instances, blindly followed them*) that both *things* and *words* came tc

* "Whose manners still our tardy apish nation,
Limps after in base imitation."—*Richard II.* ii. 1.

be sundered in form and substance. And yet does not Dan Chaucer tell us:

> "Lo, pitee renneth sone in gentil herte!"

'PROPERTY' and 'PROPRIETY,' again, are both from one root—*proprius*, *special*, *proper* (in the old sense and equivalent to the French *propre*): 'PROPERTY' is, therefore, that which is specially or peculiarly one's own; 'PROPRIETY' is the adaptation of conduct etc. to the special occasion—the instinctive perception of that course that is *proper*, fitting thereto. Among the Romans a *Patronus* was a person who had emancipated his slave, but still retained some right over him—was, as it were, a sort of *father*—pater—to him—one who was to be looked up to with veneration, and regarded as an *exemplar* which he might *copy:* 'PATRON' and 'PATTERN' are, therefore, originally one and the same word. The French verb *parler*, to speak, gives us two distinct words, 'PARLOR' and 'PARLIAMENT'—in which, however, it will not be difficult to trace the bond of union. For the 'PARLOR' (*parloir*) is properly the room in a nunnery where the nuns are permitted to meet and converse with each other—and so the common room for meeting, speaking, etc., distinct from the 'DRAWING' room, or rather the *withdrawing* room. As for 'PARLIA-

MENT,' it is preëminently the *parlementum*—the *speaking* (very often only), the *spouting* place!

We saw some time ago that 'JOURNEY' originally signified the distance travelled—dans un *jour*, in a *day*. The root is the Latin *dies*, a day. This, in the Italian, transforms itself into *giorno;* as in Dante,

> "Lo *giorno* se n'andava, e l'ær bruno
> Toglieva gli animai, che sono in terra,
> Dalle fatiche loro;" etc.
>
> *Inferno, Canto II.*

And the French, by a still further transformation, convert it into *jour:* thence it will not be difficult to perceive that a *journal* means a record of *daily* transactions. Not originally, however; for we know that in old English literature it is used in the literal sense of *daily*. As in Shakspeare,

> "Ere since the sun had made his *journal* greeting
> To the under generation."
>
> *Measure for Measure*, IV. 3.

Or in Spencer,

> "And his faint steedes watred in ocean deepe,
> Whiles from their *journall* labors they did rest."
>
> *Fairie Queene I.*, XI. 31.

But, having, as we have seen, acquired a special signification, in order to supply the deficit we went back to the Latin, and taking their adjective *diurnus* made 'DIURNAL' out of it. 'JOURNEY,' 'JOURNAL,' 'DIARY,' 'DIURNAL,' are, therefore, all from one root, the seminal force of all being *dies*, a day.

Although according to one acceptation of the word, a 'man of *honor*' may not always be a man of 'HONESTY;' yet are both these words from the same root: or rather *honestus* is properly the adjective formed from *honor* and consequently signifying the highest degree of that quality. 'HOST' and 'HOSTILE' are both from one root: and, not to dwell on the subject, so are:

PASSION	and	PASSIVE
NATURE	"	NATION
MUSTER	"	MONSTER
INGENUOUS	"	INGENIOUS
INFERIOR	"	INFERNAL
COFFER	"	COFFIN
BRAND	"	BRUNT
CUSTOM	"	COSTUME
CUPID	"	CUPIDITY
MODISH	"	MODEST, etc. etc.

From the fact of the English being a mixed language spring some curious results. One—and a very lamentable one—is, that by far the larger portion of those who speak our language—who are

"—— Native here
And to the manner born,"—

have no distinct idea of the signification of three-fourths of the words in their so called "mother tongue." Of Saxon roots we have, as it were, an innate realization: they sound like old familiar tones—snatches of melodies that we learned long, long ago; but the verbal stems from the classic tongues, and, consequently, the immense number of offshoots therefrom, seem all alien and away. And, in our heterogeneous language, how frequent are the misapplications and misunderstandings of words; and how available an opportunity does it afford for sophisms, grandiloquence and verbal quirks and quibbles of every species.*

* [Words] "being philosophically unfolded, several of those pretended mysteries, profound notions, expressed in great swelling words, whereby some were set up for reputation, being this way examined, will appear to be either nonsense, or very flat and jejune."

Bishop Wilkins: "Real Character and Philosophic Language." Epist: Dedicatory.

Archbishop Whately has observed that the double origin of our language, from Saxon and Norman material, may often enable a sophist to assume the appearance of rendering a reason, when, indeed, he is only repeating the assertion in words of a different family. Of this the following may be taken as an example: "To allow every man an unbounded freedom of speech must always be on the whole highly advantageous to the state; for (!) it is extremely conducive to the interests of the community that each individual should enjoy a liberty perfectly unlimited of expressing his sentiments."

It is interesting to observe the family of words which foreigners—according to the affinity of their language to the several elements of the English—employ. Thus a German will be sure to use 'SMEARED,' whereas a Frenchman, Spaniard, or Italian would just as certainly hit on 'ANOINTED.' So while a native of Southern Europe would naturally talk of the 'PROPINQUITY' of a place, a German would inevitably speak of its 'NEARNESS.' Saxonicus persists in speaking of the '*thoroughfaresomeness*' of stuff, in preference to the '*penetrability*' of matter; and, on the other hand, (for classical scholars are very apt, without careful pruning, to interlard the discourse too plentifully with Greek and Latin) we have heard of an Oxford fellow of a college who, on meeting a friend on horse-back, as the only way which suggested itself of asking him if it (the horse) were his *own* or *hired* or *borrowed*, demanded if it were *proprietary*, *conductitious* or *eleemosynary!**

The same peculiarity discovers itself in writers—some of whom seem to have an instinctive affinity for the Saxon element, while others are just as enamored of Latin derivatives. Thus the Saxonisms of Dean Swift and the Latinisms of Dr. Johnson are as characteristic as they are familiar. Horne Tooke has some keen and caustic passages on the neglect of developing the Teutonic element in our language, and importing so many foreign words, where native ones would do as well or better. Quaint, old Verstegan, also, has some good things on the same subject. The following for instance:—"For my own part I think them deceaved that think our speech bettered by the aboundance of our dayly borrowed woords, for they beeing of another nature and not originally belonging to our language do not, neither can they in our toung leave their natural and true deryvations: and therefore as wel may we fetch woords fro the Ethiopians or East or West Indians,† and thrust them into our

* Philological Museum.

† So we have—quite a number of them.

language and baptize all by the name of English, as those which wee dayly take from the Latin, or languages thereon depending: heer-hence it cometh (as by after experience is found) that some Englishmen discoursing together, others beeing present and of our own nation and that naturally speak the English tongue are not able to understand what the others say, notwithstanding they call it English what they speake!"*

The most amusing part in the above passage of honest Verstegan is that over a half of the words are "from the Latin, or languages thereon depending!" Let us strike the balance. A composition confined exclusively to the Saxon element, would, in all likelihood, be as stiff and unwieldy as, if totally of Latin, it would be flat or farcical. But in what admirable harmony are the several members of our great language united! With its Saxon spine and heart, animated with the breath of Latin verbs and winged with Greek substantives, it presents an organism perfect for all the purposes of practical and spiritual expression—a language "which," in the words of one of the profoundest of modern philologists, Jacob Grimm, "in wealth, good

* Restitution of Decayed Intelligence, p. 205.

sense and clearness of structure outrivals all other of the languages at this day spoken."

I am digressing, however, too far: so let us return to our Synonyms.

An interesting class of Synonyms are such as result from an exact similarity of composition, one of the pair being taken, perchance, from the Latin, the other from the Greek. Thus *natura* = phusis (φύσις), and *super* = *meta* (μετά): 'supernatural' = 'metaphysical.' *Pono* = *tithemi* (τίθημι), and *sub* = hupo (ὑπό): 'supposition' = 'hypothesis.' *Sun* (σύν) = *con*; and *metron* (μέτρον) = *mensura*: 'symmetrical' = 'commensurate.' *Con* = *sun* (σύν), and *gredior* = *ago* (ἄγω): 'congregation' = 'synagogue.' *Sus* (contracted from *sursum*) = *up*, and *teneo* = *hold*: 'sustain' = 'uphold.' *Super* = *over*, and *fluens* = *flowing*: 'superfluity' = 'overflowing.' Of these various verbal equations, each member severally is, etymologically, precisely equal to its opposite: and yet in actual use, see what a disparity frequently intervenes between them! I have mentioned 'congregation' and 'synagogue' as being, as far as derivation goes, exactly equivalent: the same may be said of 'Bible' and 'Alcoran'—the latter being Arabic for the former's Greek. And, indeed, these transcripts are often quite surprising.

'Domineer' (*dominus*, a lord) is, for instance, precisely to 'lord it over;' 'momentous' is just 'weighty;' 'trenchant' is 'cutting;' 'specious' is 'sightly;' 'pardon' is 'forgive;' 'sermon' is 'speech;' 'dictum' is a 'saying;' 'surveyor' is 'overseer; 'liberal' is 'free;' 'potent' is 'able' and 'quantity' is 'how much?' Sometimes, again, we find a dignified classicism to be just the translation of some homely piece of vernacular. Thus when we say to 'circumvent' (*circum*, around and *venio*, to come), we simply say, in Latin, to 'come round.' So, to 'connive' is literally to 'wink at;' 'punctilious' is 'pointed,' and to 'resist' is to 'take a stand against.' It is pleasant thus to discover ourselves unconscious etymologists, and bandying the same hearty idioms as resounded through the streets of Rome and Athens twenty centuries ago. Then, there is the burlesque of Synonymy—extensive domain on which I have just now no time to enter. As if, for instance, one being 'hard up' were to say that he was in a state of 'indurated loftiness,' or playfully allude to a certain enigmatical individual as the 'antique Henry.'

And new vistas open upon the suggestions of Synonyms. How profoundly significant are these correlatives often of national characteristics! What subtle glimpses do they afford into national manners and morals! The distinction, for instance, which etymologic anatomy lays bare, between the Teutonic 'banish' and the Roman 'exile' gives us an insight into certain fundamental social characteristics. For 'banish' is evidently the being subjected to the *ban*,* or proclamation—whence we gather that the French and Teutonic mode of punishment was by *public proclamation;* whereas the Latin 'exile' as clearly points to *exsilere* as its root—suggesting Cicero's definition—"perfugium potius supplicii, non supplicum."†

So in one of the triplets before given we read the various national ideas of the *commodious.* To the practical Saxon it is what is 'handy' i.e. *to his hand;* the Frenchman, however, regards it as 'suitable' (*suivre*, to follow), i.e. what naturally and properly *follows* (the necessities of the occasion?), while the Latin takes his notion thereof from, what *comes along with another*, as being its natural concomitant—and so

* This verbal root crops out through several compounds and derivatives. The '*bans* of marriage,' for example, are just the *proclamations* of marriage. So, our common phrase 'to be under *ban*,' is evidently to be under *sentence.* Furthermore, to 'abandon' is—*à (le) ban donner*—to *give* over *to the ban.* And a 'bandit' is quite as palpably one *ban-dit* ban-proclaimed, sentenced by the *ban.* Italian Bandito pl. *Banditti.*

† De Vere's Comparative Philology.

he names it 'convenient!' 'Courteous,' again, which, of course, is French born and bred, is, to the pomp-enamored Gallican that which pertains to the graces gathered at the *cour*, or court; whereas the straight-forward old Roman clustered all his ideas of the *courteous* around one to whom he could *go up and speak*—what he called homo *affabilis*, and we 'affable.'

RAMBLE ELEVENTH.

THE GROWTH OF WORDS.

"An idiom is an organism subject, like every organism, to the laws of development. One must not consider a language as a product dead and formed but once: it is an animate being and ever creative."

Wilhelm von Humboldt.

THE conception of language that has arisen prophetic on the thought of modern times is a high and great one. Speech is no more the dead mechanism it used to be conceived. Each language is a living organism; the totality of languages a grand series of organisms, all built after the same archetype, the same skeleton; but each presenting its special structural stamp, as fish, reptile, bird, mammal, are all modifications of one primitive Idea.

Yes! Language is indeed alive! Primordial creation and manifestation of the mind, Language throbs with the pulses of our life. This is the wondrous babe, begotten of the blended love of spirit and of matter—physical, mystical, the Sphinx! Through speech man realizes and incarnates himself; and Oken has an oracular utterance that "without speech there is no world."

It is one of the current wranglings, How language originated: as though Language were not an innate energy and aspiration! Language is not a cunning conventionalism arbitrarily agreed upon: it is an internal necessity. Language is not a fiction, but a truth. Language is begotten of a lustful longing to express, through the plastic vocal energy, man's secret sense of his unity with nature.

This vitality of speech manifests itself in a two-fold manifestation: in the possession of a distinctive personality and identity—in material elements and formal laws that stamp it with the stamp of linguistic individuality; and, further, in that other characteristic of every living organism—in the exhibition of growth, progress, decay—in the ongoing of processes of absorption, assimilation and elimination—in the inworking and outworking of the creative energy.

And it is in this sense that the English language is alive—as displaying successive processes of growth and development within the limits of its linguistic individuality.

The causes of that marvelous identity we call the English Language lie deep in the manifold influences that have made the English Nation. The History of a Language is measurable only in the terms of all the factors that have shaped a people's life. A nation's history is the result of the double action of internal impulses and external events. And Language expresses the infusions from all these—subtily absorbing the ethnology of a nation, its geography, government, traditions, culture, faith. Shooting its deep tap-root into eldest antiquity, drawing from the pith and sap of that grandest of all families of races and tongues—the Indo-European stock; receiving living grafts from France and Italy and Scandinavia, this divine tree of the English Speech has grown up into its sublime proportions nurtured by the history of a thousand years.

Of this superb Speech—the grandest in the world—we have no adequate treatment. There is no History of the English Language. Nor any Dictionary of the English Language. We have no such work on the English Language as the Germans possess in the "Teutonic Grammar" of Jacob Grimm, who has with masterly method and largest appreciation of modern Philology, traced the formative influences of the German speech, as it has shaped itself into conscious individuality. A History of the English Language, rising out of a full appreciation of the Philosophy of Speech (to which must go that large hospitality and impartiality that flows from the thought of the Ensemble), answering to the requirements of modern research, and after the broad, free methods America lets down, has yet to come. To the achievement of this epic work may well go the loftiest energies of both branches of the Anglican stock and speech!

How far would the Philosophy of the English Language reach! What a retrospect of ages, growths, processes, accretions, events, forces, impulses! In the motions of man's creative energy how all is interwoven with the all! How celestial forces ascend and descend and hand each other the golden pails!

An appreciation of the organic laws of the English Language in its historic unfolding is inseparable from considerations that embrace the ensemble of Languages. For ascending through the Anglo-Saxon idioms to the stock to which they belong—the Germanic or Teutonic group of tongues, we are here carried back into that grand radiation of race and speech which modern philologic criticism has formuled as the INDO-EUROPEAN line of peoples and tongues; nor do we stop till we have reached the

Persian and Indian fountains of wisdom and language. Thus it is that it is only by embracing causes, forces and impulses as old as the Japhetic man that we can rise to a full appreciation of the Philosophy of the English Language.

The Japhetites* embrace the noblest antique and later races—the Brahminic Indians, the Persians, Medians, Greeks, Romans and European peoples—theirs those noble and highly developed languages, the Sanskrit, Zend, Persian, Hellenic, Latin, Germanic, Keltic, Teutonic. In the Vedas of the Indians, especially the hymns of the Rig-Veda, and in the Zend-Avesta of the Persians—primeval documents of the Iranic world—we see the germs of all we call Europe. Here were the beginnings of the cultures of the occidental world. Science was born in that mind, the intuition of nature, the instinct for political organization and that direct practical normal conduct of life and affairs.

From this mind, too, flowered out the grandest and most spiritual of languages. The Japhetic or Iranic tongues are termed by the master-philologers the Organic Group, to distinguish them from the Agglutinative and Inorganic speech-floors that underlie them

* Sometimes termed IRANIANS or ARYANS from *Irân*, the native name of Persia.

in the Geology of Language. They alone have reached the altitude of free intellectual individuality and organism. To them belongs the splendid plasticity of Sanskrit, Greek, German, English! Such are the primeval lines in the genesis of the English language. And so it is that sounds and structures—words and forms—that were heard along the Ganges, five thousand years ago—words heard in Benares and Delhi, in Persia and Greece—are now scaling the Rocky Mountains of the Western world!

We descend. Crises present themselves in the growth of language, connected with mighty mental and social movements—crises that mark eras in History. The English—along with all the present idioms of Europe, French, Provençal, German, Italian, Spanish, Portuguese—refers itself back to that great period of ethnic flux, the few centuries succeeding the dissolution of the Roman Empire. This epoch introduces us to the birth of idioms: the laws that govern the development of language are here seen in vital play. The two elements were the German and Roman. The vigorous, individual, egotistic German, acting on the decaying Latin spoken by the remains of the Romans and by Keltic populations through France and Spain, "dissolved and as it were burst the compact structure of the Latin tongue." New forces and affinities came into action. The Teutonic genius gave its own inflections, conjugations and forms, working on Latin roots, breaking up the crystalline structure of the classic mould, freeing the grammatical forms from their absorption in the terminations of nouns and verbs, and erecting them into independent prepositions and auxiliaries. This passage from synthesis to analysis is the career of all languages. How markedly is this visible in the English! The glory of the English is that it is essentially modern—essentially unclassical.

I have shown the admirable marriage of Germanic and Roman elements present at the birth of the historical English Speech. The subsequent history of this language shows the copious infusions of new elements and the unfolding of those prolific germs, under the guidance of the influences, internal and external, that went to shape the English nation and mind.

It is this indeed which especially characterizes our tongue—its eminently composite and complex structure. It is to the scheme of Language what the diluvial rocks of the Secondary formation are in Geology. And as these have been formed by floods and inundations—water-borne and crumbling debris of antique worlds: so is the English language built out of the drift and detritus of other and elder tongues. This fact is in the line of the genius of the English race, which is unequaled in absorption and assimilation, in receptive and applicative power.

To exhibit in epic unfolding the harmonious blending of these formative elements into the grand organism of the English Language does not come within the scope of these pages. How have I longed to work on this great problem! May my aspirations some day be realized!

But within the brief limits that are left me I may have time to notice some of the most eminent contributions that have gone to the making of our language.

And first, it is needless for me to remark that the heart of our language is Anglo-Saxon. This is the spine on which the structure of our speech is hung. Drawing from the substance of the grand Germanic stock—a stock in which the instinct of personal and political independence has always been powerfully present—what infusions of passion and power and noble manly strength did our language thus receive! Saxon, too, is the whole body of grammatical forms and inflections; Saxon are the articulations—the conjunctions, articles, pronouns; Saxon those powerful instruments, the Prepositions and Auxiliaries!

And yet, had the Saxon been left to itself, it never

could have grown into the English tongue. It needed a new element. This it found in the Norman French introduced with that great political and social revolution, the Norman Conquest—a conquest that has been made the theme of much sentimental twaddle, but which was no doubt precisely the best thing that could have happened. A double action forthwith began—on the grammar and on the vocabulary, the latter copiously enriching itself with numerous terms indicative of the new political and social relations—of war, of law—of the arts and elegancies of society, which, having had no existence in Saxon life, found no utterance in the Saxon language. In regard of Grammar—of structural forms and inflections—the French influence was powerful, but indirect. Indirect, I say; because the French gave few or any forms of its own. And yet one can scarcely exaggerate the power of that influence in freeing the nascent English speech from those useless and cumbersome forms with which the Anglo-Saxon was overloaded. "The Saxon forms soon dropped away, because they did not suit the new roots; and the genius of the language, from having to deal with newly imported words in a rude state, was induced to neglect the inflexions of the native ones."* Let a single illustra-

* Jacob Grimm.

tion suffice. A complex system of the formation of the plural of nouns obtained—some nouns making that number in *a*, others in *an*, others in *as*, others in *u;* the Norman infusion, however, led to the adoption of *s* as the universal termination of all plural nouns, that being the French method and at the same time the termination of the ancient Anglo-Saxon masculine.

I have said that with the French inoculation a vast enriching of the vocabulary took place. This enriching was of course progressive—was, indeed, the work of centuries. The value of this legacy cannot be overstated: it embraced thousands of our most expressive and most important words. Of the prodigious activity with which the French genius wrought on the English language, for the four or five centuries succeeding the Conquest, we have a significant record in Chaucer. Chaucer, indeed, perhaps exaggerates the French element; and it was no doubt on account of this penchant that he in his own day received the nickname of the "French brewer." But it cannot be that Chaucer did anything more than crystallize into literature verbal forms already in solution among the floating word-capital of the day. For never otherwise could he have been the popular poet he was. What a lusty leap the English Language had taken since the Norman Conquest the Canterbury Tales vividly mirror forth. 'Twas the flush of adolescence, rich and juicy and spendthrift: manhood, compact, equable, had yet to come. Let me quote a few passages from Chaucer showing the average proportion of French in his diction. To bring it home to the eye I shall italicise the chief Norman engraftings.

Whanne that April with his showers sote
The droughte of March hath *perced* to the rote
And bathed every *veine* in swiche *licour*,
Of which *vertue engendred* is the *flour*:
Whan Zephirus eke with his sote brethe
Enspired hath in every holt and hethe
The *tendre* croppes, and the yonge sonne
Hath in the Ram his halfe *cours* yronne,
And small foules maken *melodie*,
And slepen all night with open eye,
So priketh him *nature* in his *corages*,
Than longen folk to gon on *pilgrimages*, etc.

To Canterbury with *devoute courage*,
At night was com into that *hostelrie*
Wel nine-and-twenty in a *compagnie*.

At *mortal batailles* hadde he been fiftene.

He was a *veray parfit gentil* knight.

Therfore in stede of weping and *praiers*
Men mote give silver to the poure *freres*.*

Th' *estat* th' *araie*, the *nombre* and eke the *cause*.

Were it by *aventure*, or *sort*, or *cas*.

In *prison*
Perpetuel, he n' olde no *raunsom*.

Of course amid these thousand-fold French importations many, many were not finally adopted into the vernacular. Put through the assay, they were not found fit to be stamped with the seal of popular acceptation. In Chaucer I find such Gallicisms as these—'gaillard' (gay), 'debonair' (good-natured), 'devoir' (duty), 'lointain' (the distance), 'jouissance' (enjoyment), 'misericorde' (tenderheartedness), 'pierrie' (precious stones), 'rondeur' (roundness—the 'Earth's rondeur'), with scores of such like, some of which will no doubt again make their appearance in our language, many of them expressing thoughts or things not so well expressed by any we have. But as I shall make the Unworked Mines of the English Language the theme of a future volume I shall not be tempted into farther illustration.

And now we must descend the stream of our lan-

* What we now write 'friars:' *frères*, brothers.

guage to that period when those copious tributaries from the classic fountains poured their grand affluents into the rich river of English Speech. And here we have to mention the deep debt we owe to that illustrious nation, Italy—which for so many centuries led the van of European civilization—in operating the renaissance of Greek and Latin language and thought. The breath of antique genius passed over the English mind like the air of Spring, bursting and blossoming in luxuriant growths of thought and speech. The period of this creative movement is that mighty Sixteenth century, from the reign of the Eighth Henry through the Elizabethan era. Not by hundreds merely, one may say, but by thousands, were Latin and Greek words then naturalized into the English speech.

Nor is the quality of these importations of less significance. It was theirs to satisfy the needs of the higher intellectual and spiritual expression which that new upsurging from the spontaneous depths of human nature brought. Philosophy, Science and Poetry put on that rich feuillage of verbal forms that gives such masterly expression to English literature In a word, the classical contributions furnished the spiritual conceptions, and endowed the material body of the English speech with a living soul. Under the hands of the fine geniuses of the Sixteenth and Seventeenth centuries the English Language rounded into compact, kosmic mould.

Of those three grand factors—Saxon, French, and Classical—is our language made up. It is the mutual influence and action of these that form the warp and woof of our English speech. Not but that other elements are, in greater or smaller proportions, present, and weave their threads into the divine web; but these are the main sources whence our language has enriched itself—these the main sources whether of its terms or its powers, of its material elements or its formal laws.

Of these minor tributaries the Italian, German, Norse, Portuguese, Spanish, Dutch, deserve special mention. From Italian we have such accretions as 'virtuoso,' 'bravo,' 'bandit,' 'charlatan,' 'gazette,' 'con amore,' etc. The maritime and commercial activity of the Portuguese during the Sixteenth and Seventeenth centuries has left us some significant words. Thus 'fetishism,' a term applied by them to the low idolatry and sorcery of the African tribes, is simply the Portuguese *feitico*, sorcery, witchcraft. Their relations with the African coast have also given us 'palaver'—Portuguese *palavra*, talk, speech; and applied by them to a council of African chiefs. It is, moreover, to the long monopoly by the Portuguese of the East Indian trade that we are indebted for the introduction of various oriental words, as 'taboo' from the Sandwich Islands, and the phrase 'run-*amuck*' from the Malays. The Dutch have left the impress of their maritime activity on our language. 'Sloop,' for instance, and 'yacht' and 'schooner' are all of Dutch etymology. To later German we owe the suggestions of many valuable metaphysical symbols, made after the antique—not the least significant of which are the much-used 'objective' and 'subjective.' Nor is this all, there being scarce a tongue on the planet which the all-absorbing Saxon genius has not laid under contribution to enrich the exchequer of its conquering speech. The aboriginal American dialects, for instance, have given us 'tobacco,' 'wigwam,' 'papouse,' 'moccasin,' 'Yankee,' 'potato,' 'chocolate,' and others. The Slaves have contributed 'plough,' word and thing. Arabia shows her powerful influence on the culture of the Middle Ages in such terms as 'algebra,' 'zero,' 'almanach,' 'alkali,' 'alembic,' 'elixir,' 'alcohol,' etc. Hebraisms, too, are not lacking—witness 'sabbath,' 'jubilee,' 'hallelujah,' 'amen,' 'cabala,' 'Messiah,' etc. Turkey sends us 'tulip,' 'turban,' 'dragoman;' Persia, 'bazaar,' 'caravan,' 'azure,' 'scarlet;' China, 'tea' and 'Nankeen;' Hindostan, 'calico, 'chintz,' 'curry,' 'lac;' the Malays 'bantam,' 'gamboge,' 'rattan,' 'sago.'

The growth of words runs parallel with the unfolding of a nation's life. Every addition to practical civilization, every scientific generalization, commerce in all its branches, foreign literary influence, diplomacy, religion, philosophy, sociology are the perpetual agents of linguistic increase.

A curious law attaches to the origin of words by which they are forced to undergo a period of probationship before they receive the stamp of legal currency. Every new word passes through an embryonic stage previous to emerging as a normal member of the organism of speech, and perhaps for half a century or more finds a place in no dictionary. The advent of every neologism is met by a powerful conservatism opposing the innovation: and only after a severe ordeal does it raise itself to a place in the peerage of language. With its emergence in the Dictionary it has passed the grand climacteric, and may henceforth count on a longer or shorter lease of life. Thousands of words, too, make their debut as slang—gipseys and outlaws that are afterwards reclaimed by civilized society. And it is curious to observe how many of our stateliest terms rest on some free popular idiom, some bandied catch-word—spontaneous creation of the hour.

In the Essays of Montaigne there is a vivid illustration of the subtle steps by which words often find their way into language. In order to facilitate his acquisition of Latin, then the common speech of the learned, he was, in his childhood, allowed no other medium of communication; and not only his teachers, but his parents, attendants, and even his nurse, were obliged to learn enough Latin to converse with him in it. The result was, as he tells us, that the peasants on his father's estate, and gradually the people of the neighboring villages, adopted many of the Latin words which they heard constantly used in the family of their feudal lord; and, writing fifty years later, he declares that these words had become permanently incorporated into the dialect of the province.

'Mob' is a word that made its appearance in the English language in the time of Charles II. as a piece of pure slang, and I have already quoted from the Spectator characterizing it as a ridiculous expression which might however finally make its way into our language! How long did 'bore' struggle to maintain its hold! It expressed, however, a positive idea, not otherwise conveyed, and has finally, in our own time, won its way into the Dictionary. You look in vain in any vocabulary of the English language for 'sociology' (creation of Auguste Comte) 'solidarity,' 'placer:' they are all most valuable contributions, however, and will no doubt soon receive Dictionary-endorsement. 'Telegram' again, which appears in the new editions of the English dictionaries, is an example of how an imperious necessity will force words into immediate acceptance and recognition.

The French contributions to our language, so copious and rich, were never more important than they have been within the present century. Let me enumerate some that we have received within that period, with others that look a little farther back. I shall give such as suggest themselves to my mind, without any attempt at completeness.

Accoucheur—Accouchement: Valuable contributions to our language, and now getting into popular use.

Attaché: A diplomatic term, implying one *attached* to the suite of an embassador, and now creeping into more general use. Thus we speak about the *attachés* of a reigning belle.

Au fait: "Posted up"—up to the mark, having an off-hand familiarity with the matter in hand.

Badinage: Half-earnest jesting—a delicate modification of raillery.

Blasé: Past participle of the verb *blaser*, to surfeit, and popularized by the comedy of "Used Up."

Bon-mot or simply *Mot:* Literally a *good word*—a good thing.

Brochure: A pamphlet: from the verb *brocher*, to stitch.

Coup: A stroke or blow, and in compounds implies any sudden action. The compounds are very numerous, *coup-d'état*, *coup-de-grace*, *coup-de-main*, *coup-de-soleil*, *coup-d'œil*, *coup-de-théâtre*, etc.

Debris: A symbolism from Geology, where it means masses of rock etc., detached by attrition or mechanical violence.

Debut: First public appearance. *Debutant*, *Debutante*, the person making it.

Elite: The flower—literally the *elect* or *chosen*.

Employé: A word of the greatest utility and coming into universal use: the meaning is any one *employed*.

Ennui: Weariness, sense of tedium.

Ensemble: The totality as distinguished from the details. A noble word with immense vista.

Façade: Chief *frontage* of a building—a term borrowed from the French architects.

Goût: Relish, æsthetic taste.

Naïve, Naïveté: Most desirable words, with the French elisive charm, and implying a combination of the ingenuous, candid, winning.

Nonchalance: Cool carelessness and indifference.

Outré: Etymologically the same as *ultra* and carrying with it the sense of the extravagant and grotesque.

Passé: A term whose import is realized with tremendous force by ladies of a certain age. *En passant*, by the way.

Penchant: Inclination, proclivity.

Persiflage: Light, mocking banter.

Personnel: Originally, corps of *persons* employed in contradistinction to the *materiel;* but now coming to mean, also, the sum of characteristics constituting one's personality.

Précis: A summary or abridgment. A valuable word.

Prestige: A most useful word, supplying a positive want in our language. The original meaning was a piece of smuggling or imposture; but the word now bears with it the idea of *the presumption which past successes beget of future ones.*

Programme: A word of universal use in America in the sense of a printed synopsis: a desirable contribution, which the French has given us, taking it from the Greek.

Protegé: One under the patronage or protection of another—Roman *clients.*

Rapport: Implies, in French, *relation; en rapport,* in relation with; and used in English to convey the idea of an affinity or sympathy of sensation. The word owes its currency to our modern mesmeric and "Spiritual" phenomena and philosophy.

Redacteur: An editor, compiler etc.; *redaction,* the digesting or reducing to order literary or scientific material.

Renaissance: Regeneration, new birth: mainly applied to the revival of the fine arts, but susceptible of any breadth of application.

Séance: A sitting, applied mostly to sittings for scientific purposes.

Soirée: A word early adopted, and after the analogy of which we have more recently introduced *matinée.*

RAMBLE TWELFTH.

ENGLISH IN AMERICA.

BY a combination of circumstances the English Language became the speech of America. There was nothing fortuitous in this. For English is eminently the speech of the Modern. The English Language expresses most typically those tendencies which all show more or less. Into the make of the English, more than any other idiom, has converged the spirit of the modern, breaking up the crystalline structure of the classic mould—the splendid newness, the aspirations of freedom, individualism, democracy.

Nurtured by the influences that have made the English nation, the English Language expresses the infusions from all these—expresses aristocracy and monarchy among the rest. Meanwhile do we not feel that a change has, these eras, passed over the private spirit of man? The genius of a new age broods, fiery and fecundating, over the nations. Authority tradition, caste go hopelessly. New tests, demands, verdicts come, disconcerting the old decorums in opinions, manners, literature. Audacious aspirations arise. A lofty augury beckons on to new cerebral and spiritual shores.

A speech to correspond! These oceanic movements in the age must make flood-tide in the Language, also. For speech moves with the movements of mind, as the ocean obeys celestial influences. Always Language is incubated by the mind of the ages. Transported to the new and vaster arena of America, the English language comes under the conditions, outer and inner, that are shaping the American mind. It is qualified by all that makes American life—by the geographic and climatic conditions, by the ethnology of America, by her politics, sociology, manners, mentality.

Of course the English Language must take on new powers in America. And here we are favored by the genius of this grand and noble language, which more than all others lends itself plastic and willing to the moulding power of new formative influences. Was it supposed that the English Language was finished? But there is no finality to a Language! The English has vast vista in it—vast vista in America.

It is the sum of the uses of precedents, to a live nation, that it shall match the same with better from its own soul, and consume them before its audacious improvisations. A nation cannot live on reminiscences: it can only live on influx. The English Language, expressing the genius of the English race and its culture history, thought, is still inadequate to the utterance of America, and must take on new proportions before it can become the living garment of this new life of humanity.

The future expansions of the English Language in America are already marked in the great lines of development this idiom shows. It is for us freely to follow the divine indications. And here a spinal fact is the composite character of our language: to what new realizations is it lifted in America! The immense diversity of race, temperament, character—the copious streams of humanity constantly flowing hither—must reappear in free, rich growths of speech. From no one ethnic source is America sprung: the electric reciprocations of many stocks conspired and conspire. This opulence of race-elements is in the theory of America. Land of the Ensemble, to her the consenting currents flow, and the ethnology of the States draws the grand outline of that hospitality and reception that must mark the new politics, sociology, literature and religion.

Language, too, must feel this influence. And this is to appear not merely in the copious new verbal contributions the various idioms may bring, but in the entire spirit of the Language—moulded more and more to a large hospitality and impartiality. The theory of English scholars and literateurs, for hundreds of years, has been the theory of repression. They have discouraged and cramped the spontaneous expansions of the Language—discouraged inoculations from the French, from Latin, Greek, Italian. What pitiful cant, too, does one hear every day about Saxon! as though it were not the very theory of the English Language—the very genius and animus of it—to take its food from all sources! This ridiculous nonsense is to be utterly dismissed.

What starvation has this insane purism effected! What a poor, indigent, watery affair is our literary expression! Books cling to the old traditions and timidities—no full, free, utterance, untrammeled, mystical: no influx, no abandonment. Surely the time has come to dismiss this old impotence. And what means arise for enriching the arsenal of expression! What new creations surge and swell the ampler currents of our time! New thoughts, new things, all unnamed! Where is the theory of literary expression that stands for the new politics and soci ology? that puts itself abreast the vast divine tendencies of Science? that absorbs the superb suggestions of the Grand Opera?

I can see but one limitation to the theory of Words—the theory of Things. Is it for us who are borne on the billowy tides of this new humanity to limit the unfolding opulence of God—to put a girdle round the widening future of our civilization and our speech? Freely, then, may the American literat proceed to quarry and build in the architecture of the English Language. Of course the conditions of this free expressive activity are high. To him who would mould our language must go many qualities—must go large knowledge of the philosophy of speech, must go rich æsthetic instincts, among the rest.

The sources of future enrichings of the Anglican speech are the same old fountains. In our native roots, in the plastic forms of the antique, in the noble modern idioms are the magazines of word-wealth. How much has the French language been to English! How much has it yet to give! Nation of sublime destinies, noble, naïve, rich with humanity, bearers of freedom, upholding on her shoulders the history of Europe for a thousand years! The Italian gifts, too, direct and indirect, are not nothing to America. Spain is not nothing. How much they have to contribute—Italy with her rich and rosy nature, her grand style of music and consummate intuitions of art; Spain, so noble, so proud, so much to manners, to behavior! I would not underrate the German and Scandinavian influences—mighty race, spiritual, aspiring, individual, melancholy, prudent.

The flower and aroma of a Nation is its Language. The conditions of a grand language are a grand life. For words are metaphysical beings, and draw of the life of the mind. Not in these wondrous hieroglyphs of Words, not in these mystic runes, is the power: in the Mind which loads these airy messengers with burdens of meaning is the vis and vivification of speech. Over the transformations of a Language the genius of a nation unconsciously presides—the issues of Words represent issues in the national thought. And in the vernal seasons of a nation's life the formative energy puts forth verbal growths opulent as flowers in spring.

THE END.

INDEX.

www.ingramcontent.com/pod-product-compliance
Lightning Source LLC
LaVergne TN
LVHW020239110826
845151LV00003B/973

9781425529390